Counseling Persons
with Addictions
& Compulsions

A Handbook for Clergy
and Other Helping Professionals

**Andrew J. Weaver,
Charlene Hosenfeld,
and Harold G. Koenig**

THE
PILGRIM
PRESS
Cleveland

To my brother in Christ, Ray McGovern — AJW
To my husband, Rollo Scheurenbrand — CAH
To my son, Jordan Koenig — HGK

The Pilgrim Press
700 Prospect Avenue
Cleveland, Ohio 44115-1100
thepilgrimpress.com

✤ Printed in the United States of America on acid-free paper that contains
   30% post-consumer fiber.

12 11 10 09 08 07   5 4 3 2 1

Library of Congress Cataloging-in-Publication Data

Weaver, Andrew J., 1947-
    Counseling persons with addictions and compulsions : a handbook for clergy and other helping professionals / Andrew J. Weaver, Charlene A. Hosenfeld, Harold G. Koenig.
       p.   cm.
    Includes index.
    ISBN 978-0-8298-1705-8 (alk. paper)
    1. Pastoral counseling. 2. Addicts – Pastoral counseling of. 3. Substance abuse – Religious aspects – Christianity. 4. Compulsive behavior – Religious aspects – Christianity. I. Hosenfeld, Charlene A., 1950- II. Koenig, Harold George. III. Title.
    BV4460.W427 2007
    259′.429 – dc22
                                                                    2006036277

Counseling Persons with Addictions & Compulsions

Contents

Foreword

L ittle did I know when I started my ministry almost 20 years ago that the challenges of each new day would so test my ability to respond in meaningful ways to the countless problems faced by my parishioners.

I doubt that I was so different from many young pastors who, having graduated from seminary, feel competent, confident, and qualified to meet the everyday needs of life in the church.

Nor do I believe that I was the only one who quickly established that I had more to learn about how to provide meaningful ministry to the people I was called to serve than my good seminary education had given me.

Very little that I can recall from my days in seminary — intense as they were — prepared me for the terrified parent who got a call from the emergency room saying her son was near death following a drug overdose; for the young man whose life was torn apart because, while he was driving under the influence of alcohol, he lost control of the car and his two teenage passengers were killed; for the husband who could not keep the promise to his wife that he would quit using chewing tobacco; or for the child abused continuously by his alcoholic father.

Over the years I have learned how utterly commonplace it is for religious leaders to find themselves in situations with their communities in which they feel overwhelmed and ill-equipped to meet the challenges of the day. And yet those leaders must nonetheless meet each of those challenges with knowledge and wisdom, with grace and dignity, and with the best information they have at hand.

Many times in ministry I did not meet those challenges well. Either I was too stubborn or too arrogant to realize that I was in a situation in which a parishioner should have been referred to professionally trained experts, or I was ignorant of how to provide such resources, or what I was hearing was so far beyond my experience that I felt I could be of no use whatsoever.

Eventually, I began a long and arduous process of continuing education that better equipped me to respond in appropriate ways to the challenges I faced as a local church pastor. I learned much about what to say and, more importantly, what not to say in certain situations. I thirsted for the kinds of resources that would equip me as a local church pastor to piece together the broken lives of those who found the courage to reach out for help in some of the most desperate of circumstances.

One of the most important things I learned was that, while the gift of referral to professionals could make the difference between a person in distress coping or not, that did not release from me my own responsibilities to provide at least some initial spiritual guidance and comfort to those who had sought my help. Indeed, the church as a body itself broken and made whole by the love of God is a solace that many have found essential as they wrestle with their demons.

Which is all to say that I wish the resource for which I am writing this foreword had been available to me upon my graduation from seminary and ordination. It was with great joy that I read through the manuscript I had been given, all the while saying to myself: "Where was this 20 years ago?" It should be a required desk reference for all leaders of faith communities and especially all who counsel and offer pastoral care.

In very simple language, each chapter presents essential information about easily misunderstood challenges faced by many of those in our faith communities. Its diagnostic material helps to remove the stain of embarrassment often felt acutely by members who fear the judgment of their fellow members, many of whom they fantasize about being more righteous than they are.

The authors present case studies rooted in concrete circumstances to which most pastors can easily relate. In addition to the characteristics of the presenting challenge, the outline and analysis of the pastor's response and assessment provide readers with good information about appropriate ways in which they too can respond.

A recital of the relevant history in each case study is a useful touch. Too often, those coming to us for counsel and care share information that does not necessarily bear on the matter at hand, and being able to separate the significant from the distracting is a gift. I am grateful for the work of those trained professionals who can do that and for the opportunity in this resource to read their reports. Beyond being interesting reading, it reinforces my belief that there are and will always be limits beyond which the untrained pastor should not go. Some matters really are best left to the specialists.

I am grateful that a piece of each case study includes an analysis of ways in which treatment can be supported or added to by the faith community. As I said earlier, making referrals is not a way to ignore or evade our own responsibilities as healers. And while knowing the limits of what we are capable is essential to any healing process, knowing also the ways in which faith communities can partner with trained mental health professionals is highly beneficial. The suggestions offered in this part of the material are among the most important in this resource and are a part of what makes this more than just a textbook on the presenting symptoms.

Finally, as one whose doctoral studies were focused on white privilege in the church, I am especially grateful for the ways in which cross-cultural issues are addressed by the authors. We should not presume that all cultures respond to or interpret stimuli in the same way. Nor should we assume that the only ones we will be called upon to serve are those whose challenges arise from within the same culture in which we currently reside.

It is long past due that a book like this be published. Pastors, rabbis, other leaders of faith communities, and those in training for such positions would be wise to add it to those select few books they keep on their desk. That next phone call or office visit may be one that requires of them more than that for which their seminary training has prepared them.

Rev. Dr. John Dorhauer

Rev. Dr. John Dorhauer is Associate Conference Minister for the Missouri Mid-South Conference of the United Church of Christ and worked directly with youth for the first 16 years of his ministry. He has counseled many young people who have struggled with alcohol and drug abuse, and has counseled high school students who have lost friends to such abuse.

Acknowledgments

We are grateful to the Reverend Carolyn L. Stapleton, who serves at the Chinese United Methodist Church in New York City, for her exceptional editing and research skills that added immeasurably to the quality and usefulness of the text. We are also appreciative of the assistance of Suk Ki Lee for her help in preparing the manuscript.

Whither shall I go from thy Spirit?
Or whither shall I flee from thy presence?
If I ascend to heaven, thou art there!
If I make my bed in Sheol, thou art there!
If I take the wings of the morning
and dwell in the uttermost parts of the sea,
even there thy hand shall lead me,
and thy right hand shall hold me.
If I say, "Let only darkness cover me,
and the light about me be night,"
even the darkness is not dark to thee,
the night is bright as the day;
for darkness is as light with thee.

—Psalm 139:7–12 RSV

How to Use This Book

Counseling Persons with Addictions: A Handbook for Pastors and Other Helping Professionals is designed to be a text for those in training for pastoral ministry as well as a useful resource for clergy and other professionals who encounter a wide array of addictions and compulsions. The volume deals with such issues as addiction to alcohol, gambling, tobacco, cocaine, inhalants, over-the-counter drugs, prescription drugs, steroids, and methamphetamines, as well as compulsive shopping, exercise, computer use, and eating. In this period of widespread concern with addictions and compulsions, it is especially important that pastors and others in ministry understand how to help guide persons through these issues.

Part 1 offers information about the important role that clergy and the faith community serve in the mental health care of addicted persons and their families. This section spells out the need for special expertise by pastors and other religious professionals in how to recognize and address these conditions. This part of the book outlines the latest research-based information about how individuals and families use religion to prevent addictions from arising, as well as how faith can help them cope with the emotional distress related to these issues.

The heart of the book is found in Part 2. It is presented in a format that uses real-life situations while highlighting practical implications for pastoral care. These case studies reflect the current knowledge available on each of 17 separate topics. The case studies make use of a multi-disciplinary approach that integrates up-to-date clinical knowledge in pastoral care, psychology, psychiatry, nursing, and social work, along with contemporary scientific findings on the role of religion in mental health care.

The book is designed so that a reader can easily locate information on addictions and related mental health problems for which individuals and families seek pastoral counsel. It is an easy-to-use guide that provides for clergy and others the accurate and practical information they need on addictions when parishioners come to them seeking counsel.

We include in each chapter information about how a pastor or colleague in ministry would assess the problem, what aspects of the case are most important, how to identify the major issues, specific directions about what a pastor and congregation can do, when to refer for professional assistance, and information about resources that can provide help. For each concern addressed we identify national organizations (often with toll-free numbers and Internet addresses) that supply information and support for families facing these issues. Cross-cultural aspects are noted and discussed, as well. We define technical terms in the glossary at the end of the book.

The text is written for people of all faiths, and with an appreciation for the richness of the intergenerational and multicultural diversity found in religious communities. The authors are people of faith with specialties in mental health.

Dr. Weaver is a clinical psychologist and ordained United Methodist minister who has served rural and urban parishes. He has written over 160 scientific articles and book chapters and has co-authored 12 books. Dr. Hosenfeld is a Presbyterian laywoman and licensed clinical psychologist in Hawaii who has a private practice and also works in a hospital setting. She has more than 24 years of clinical experience and has worked with numerous clients who suffer from addictions. Dr. Koenig, an evangelical Christian, is professor of psychiatry and internal medicine, as well as director of the Center for Religion/Spirituality and Health at Duke University Medical Center. He has written over 200 scientific articles and book chapters and has authored or co-authored 30 books.

PART ONE

Introduction

Addictions, Clergy, and Faith

ddiction is a problem that ranks among the top health and social issues in the United States. According to the Substance Abuse and Mental Health Services (SAMHSA) 2002 survey, 120 million Americans aged 12 and older consume alcohol. About 54 million binge drink and 15.9 million are heavy drinkers. An estimated 19.5 million Americans aged 12 and older abuse illicit drugs. Marijuana is the most commonly used illegal drug with 14.6 million users, about one-third of whom used it on 20 or more days in the preceding month. There are 2 million cocaine users, of whom 567,000 use crack cocaine. There are also an estimated 166,000 heroin addicts (SAMHSA, 2003).

Among youth aged 12 to 17 years, 11.6 percent are illicit drug users. The rate of use is even higher among young adults (18 to 25 years) at 20 percent (SAMHSA, 2003). A large number of high school seniors have tried marijuana (42 percent), inhalants (17 percent), LSD (12 percent), and cocaine (6 percent). This is of particular concern because the greatest risk of developing a long-term substance abuse problem occurs in the teenage years (Burke et al., 1990).

Annually, drug and alcohol abuse contributes to the death of more than 120,000 Americans. In 2002, an estimated 11 million individuals reported having driven under the influence of alcohol or an illicit drug during the past year (SAMHSA, 2003). Drugs and alcohol cost Americans more than $294 billion annually in preventable expenses and lost productivity. The largest number of admissions for illicit drug treatment are for cocaine (38 percent), followed by heroin (25 percent) and marijuana (19 percent), according to the National Association of State Alcohol and Drug Abuse Directors (1997).

Tobacco use is associated with the increased likelihood of using other addictive substances, acting for many as a "gateway drug" (Elders et al., 1994). About 71.5 million Americans aged 12 and older use tobacco. Each day nearly 3,000 American youth begin smoking (An et al., 1999). It is estimated that between one-third and one-half of adolescents who try only a few cigarettes will become regular smokers (Henningfield et al., 1991).

Ecstasy, or MDMA (an acronym for its chemical name: 3,4-methyl-enedioxymethamphetamine), is an example of a new drug that has become widely used in recent years (SAMHSA, 2003). It is an illegal substance that acts as both a stimulant and hallucinogen, producing an energizing effect, as well as distortions in time and perception and enhanced enjoyment of tactile experiences. In 2002, over 10 million persons aged 12 and older reported using Ecstasy at least once, up from 6.4 million in 2000. In the United States, Ecstasy use has been rising steadily since 1992 (SAMHSA, 2003).

Problem gambling is another addictive behavior that is showing a sharp increase. Americans spend more annually on wagering than on movies, sporting events, concerts, and theater combined (Vogel, 1997). Experts argue that for some individuals gambling is no less potent that heroin or cocaine and that it is the fastest growing addiction in the United States (Freiberg, 1995). It is estimated that there are at least 4 million problem gamblers in the United States. Persons become preoccupied with gambling, seeking the "high" of betting through increasing the amounts of money they wager.

People with Addictions Seek Clergy Counsel

It is important that clergy be skilled in recognizing addictions, given the size of the problem in our nation. Research over several decades has demonstrated that millions of Americans call upon clergy for help in times of trouble, which includes dealing with problems related to addiction (Weaver, 1995). Pastors are often in long-term relationships with individuals and their families which enable them to observe changes in behavior that may indicate early signs of addiction (Weaver, Revilla, and Koenig, 2002). Furthermore, clergy are accessible helpers within communities that offer a sense of continuity with centuries of human history. Congregations also have established patterns of responding to crises. Pastors can help mental health professionals gain access to persons with problems who would otherwise not receive needed psychological care.

A University of Michigan research group published results of a survey using a national sample of Americans. The study found that about four in ten of them reported that they sought counsel from a member of the clergy when they had a personal problem. Among people who stated they attended religious services once a week, the number rose to 53 percent (Veroff, Kulka, and Douvan, 1981).

The U.S. Surgeon General's recent *Report on Mental Health* found that each year one of six adults and one of five children obtain mental health services from one of the following: a health care provider, a clergyperson, a social services agency, or a school (Satcher, 2000). The 353,000 Christian and Jewish clergy serving congregations in the United States (4,000 rabbis; 49,000 Catholic priests; and 300,000 Protestant ministers, according to the U.S. Department of Labor, 1998) are among the most trusted professionals in society (Gallup and Lindsay, 1999).

Researchers at Yale University surveyed Catholic, Protestant, and Jewish clergy in New Haven, Connecticut. A majority of those clergy reported that they had counseled persons with drug and alcohol problems, while African-American pastors reported that they "had twice as much counseling experience with drug and alcohol abuse" as others in the study. These authors summarized their findings with the statement: "Parish-based clergy, especially the black clergy, function as a major mental health resource to communities with limited access to professional mental health services" (Mollica et al., 1986, p. 323).

The church and clergy serve as an important resource within the African-American community for persons with problems (Neighbors et al., 1998). In an extensive study of 635 African-American congregations in the northern United States, 54 percent of the ministers "considered drug abuse the most serious problem in their community" (Thomas et al., 1994). Church programs related to this issue included drug abuse counseling, drug education, and sponsorship of Alcoholics Anonymous and Narcotics Anonymous groups. Researchers interviewed 121 African-American pastors in 99 churches in Connecticut. Two of three clergy said they had significant numbers of persons with substance abuse problems in their congregations (Young et al., 2003). Ninety-four of the churches offered community outreach programs for those in need. One in three of the congregations offered services to persons who suffer from substance abuse (Williams et al., 1999).

Researchers asked rabbis and Protestant ministers in Southern California to name training areas in which they could use the most help among 14 choices. The rabbis identified training in alcohol/drug problems as the number one issue while the Protestant pastors named it the second most important area for additional training, a little behind parenting concerns (Ingram and Lowe, 1989; Lowe, 1986). In a survey of European-American and African-American clergy in Memphis, Tennessee, researchers asked about their level of confidence as counselors in seven areas. Drug and alcohol problems ranked second to last among the seven areas in which the clergy felt confident to counsel (Mannon and Crawford, 1996).

Other professionals see pastors as important community resources who offer valuable counsel to those in need. A survey of the American Academy of Family Physicians found that more than eight in ten referred or recommended their patients to clergy for counseling. About one in five of the physicians listed substance abuse as the reason for their patient referral to clergy (Daaleman and Frey, 1998).

The University of Texas Medical Center in Galveston surveyed 75 percent of the pastors in its community (Turner, 1995). It found no ongoing programs in congregations for addicted persons, while a majority of the clergy expressed interest in learning more about addictions and enhancing their skills as counselors. The University Medical Center co-sponsored with local clergy a monthly seminar offering such topics as spiritual needs of persons in recovery, 12-step programs, and the physician's role in treating addiction. This proved to be a highly successful collaboration between health professionals and religious leaders that has improved addiction treatment in that community (Turner, 1995).

An alliance of African-American churches in rural Virginia, in an effort to address health issues, began a smoking cessation program. It combined one-on-one counseling with self-help materials and community-wide activities (Voorhees et al., 1996). It demonstrated how a smoking cessation intervention for African-Americans can be successfully implemented through a church coalition. Faith-based tobacco-cessation programs focused on minority groups that suffer a disproportionately higher burden of tobacco-attributable illnesses and deaths may be of particular value (Voorhees et al., 1996).

Faith's Role in the Prevention of Addictions among Adolescents

Research findings consistently support the conclusion that public and private religious involvement can act as protective factors that decrease the probability that a young person will use illicit drugs (Wills et al., 2003). Faith communities offer supportive environments that can reinforce family attitudes and teachings against substance abuse. Commitment to a nurturing religious community may also offer a purpose in life that makes drug use less attractive. Increased family and teen faith involvement has been linked to lower levels of substance abuse and to negative attitudes toward substance use in diverse populations in the United States (Blyth and Leffert, 1995; Brody et al., 1996; Yarnold and Patterson, 1995).

One study in the United States examined a sample of 13,250 students in grades 7 to 12 (Bahr et al., 1993). The researchers found that the greater the religious involvement, the less likely it is that a teen will use alcohol, marijuana, amphetamines, or depressants. Adolescents who are involved in faith-based activities are also less likely to have friends who use alcohol and illicit drugs.

A second study compared 112 towns and cities in which 33,397 high school students lived. It measured 16 problem behaviors in seven areas: tobacco use, sexual activity, alcohol use, depression and suicide, illicit drug use, anti-social behaviors, and school problems. Communities with a majority of high school students attending religious services at least once a month were half as likely to be among the communities with the most problem behaviors, including addictions among youth (Blyth and Leffert, 1995).

When considering the risk factors for using "crack" cocaine among adolescents in Miami, Florida, researchers found that religious involvement was a strong predictor of lowered "crack" use after controlling for ten separate factors including: family background, structure, and relationships; peer associations and influences; and school history (Yarnold and Patterson, 1995). Arizona high school students who were not religious were almost twice as likely to use marijuana than were their religious counterparts (Hardert and Dowd, 1994).

In Great Britain, a study involving 4,753 adolescents found that religious belief and practice had a strong association with a young person's negative attitudes toward substance abuse, including the use of marijuana, alcohol, glue, heroin, butane gas, and tobacco (Francis and Mullen, 1993).

Summary

This book addresses a number of issues of concern to clergy and to those who come to them for guidance with addictions. These are problems that religious professionals and pastors are called upon to respond to within congregations and communities, often with inadequate information. Given the size of the problem, one can assume that there will be a continued need for ministers, priests, sisters, rabbis, imams, and other religious professionals to offer informed help. There is a real need for them to learn how to competently recognize addictive processes, identify when to make referrals to mental health clinicians, help persons find available community resources, and train members of their congregations to provide support to affected individuals and families.

References

American Psychiatric Association. (2000). *Diagnostic and statistical manual of mental disorders* (4th ed., text revision). Washington, DC: American Psychiatric Association.

An, L. C., O'Malley, P. M., Schulenberg, J., Bachman, J. G., and Johnston, L. D. (1999). Changes at the high end of risk in cigarette smoking among US high school seniors. *American Journal of Public Health,* 89(5), 699–705.

Bahr, S. J., Hawk, R. D., and Wang, G. (1993). Family and religious influences on adolescent substance abuse. *Youth and Society,* 24(4), 443–465.

Blyth, D. A., and Leffert, N. (1995). Communities as contexts for adolescent development: An empirical analysis. *Journal of Adolescence Research,* 10(1), 64–87.

Brody, G. H., Stoneman, Z., and Flor, D. (1996). Parental religiosity, family processes, and youth competence in rural, two-parent African-American families. *Developmental Psychology,* 32, 696–706.

Burke, K. E., Burke, J. D., Regier, D. A., and Rea, D. S. (1990). Age at onset of selected mental disorders in five community populations. *Archives of General Psychiatry, 47,* 511–518.

Daaleman, T. P., and Frey, B. (1998). Prevalence and patterns of physicians' referral to clergy and pastoral care providers. *Archives of Family Medicine, 7,* 548–553.

Elders, M. J., Perry, C. L., Eriksen, M. P., and Giovino, G. A. (1994). The report of the surgeon general: Preventing tobacco use among young people. *American Journal of Public Health,* 84(4), 543–547.

Francis, L. J., and Mullen, K. (1993). Religiosity and attitudes toward drug use among 13–15 year olds in England. *Addiction, 88,* 665–672.

Freiberg, P. (1995). Pathological gambling turning into epidemic. *American Psychological Association Monitor,* December issue. Washington, DC: American Psychological Association.

Gallup, G. H., and Lindsay, D. M. (1999). *Surveying the religious landscape: Trends in U.S. beliefs.* Harrisburg, PA: Morehouse Publishing.

Hardert, R. A., and Dowd, T. J. (1994). Alcohol and marijuana use among high school and college students in Phoenix, Arizona: A test of Kandel's socialization theory. *International Journal of Addictions,* 29(7), 887–912.

Henningfield, J. E., Cohen, C., and Slade, J. D. (1991). Is nicotine more addictive than cocaine? *British Journal of Addiction, 86,* 565–569.

Ingram, B. L., and Lowe, D. (1989). Counseling activities and referral practices of rabbis. *Journal of Psychology and Judaism, 13,* 133–148.

Lowe, D. W. (1986). Counseling activities and referral practices of ministers. *Journal of Psychology and Christianity, 5,* 22–29.

Mannon, J. D., and Crawford, R. L. (1996). Clergy confidence to counsel and their willingness to refer to mental health professionals. *Family Therapy,* 23(3), 213–231.

Mollica, R. C., Streets, F. J., Boscarino, J., and Redlich, F. C. (1986). A community study of formal pastoral counseling activities of the clergy. *American Journal of Psychiatry*, 143, 323–328.

National Association of State Alcohol and Drug Abuse Directors. (1997). *State resources and services related to alcohol and other drug problems for fiscal year 1995: An analysis of state alcohol and drug abuse profile data*. Washington, DC: National Association of State Alcohol and Drug Abuse Directors.

Neighbors, H. W., Musick, M. A., and Williams, D. R. (1998). The African American minister as a source of help for serious personal crises: Bridges or barriers to mental health care? *Health Education and Behavior*, 25(6), 759–777.

Satcher, D. (2000). Mental health: A report of the Surgeon General – executive summary. *Professional Psychology: Research and Practice*, 31(1), 13–15.

Substance Abuse and Mental Health Services Administration (SAMHSA) (2003). *Overview of findings from the 2002 national survey on drug use and health* (Office of Applied Studies, NHSDA Series H-21, DHHS Publication No. SMA 03-3774). Rockville, MD.

Thomas, S. B., Quinn, S. C., Billingsley, A., and Caldwell, C. (1994). The characteristics of northern black churches with community health outreach programs. *American Journal of Public Health*, 84, 575–579.

Turner, W. H. (1995). Bridging the gap: Addressing alcohol and drug addiction from a community health perspective. *American Journal of Public Health*, 85(6), 870–871.

United States Department of Labor. (1998). *Occupational outlook handbook: United States Department of Labor*. Washington, DC: Bureau of Labor Statistics.

Veroff, J., Kulka, R. A., and Douvan, E. (1981). *Mental health in America: Patterns of help-seeking from 1957 to 1976*. New York: Basic Books.

Vogel, J. (1997). *Crapped out: How gambling ruins the economy and destroys lives*. Monroe, ME: Common Courage Press.

Voorhees, C. C., Stillman, F. A., Swank, R. T., Heagerty, P. J., Levine, D. M., and Becker, D. M. (1996). Heart, body, and soul: Impact of church-based smoking cessation interventions on readiness to quit. *Preventive Medicine, 25*(3), 277–285.

Weaver, A. J. (1995). Has there been a failure to prepare and support parish-based clergy in their role as front-line community mental health workers? A review. *Journal of Pastoral Care, 49*, 129–149.

Weaver, A. J., Koenig, H. G., and Larson, D. B. (1997). Marital and family therapists and the clergy: A need for clinical collaboration, training and research. *Journal of Marital and Family Therapy, 23*(1), 13–25.

Weaver, A. J., Revilla, L. A., and Koenig, H. G. (2002). *Counseling families across the stages of life: A handbook for pastors and other helping professionals*. Nashville: Abingdon Press.

Williams, D. R., Griffins, E. H., Young, J. L., Collins, C., and Dobson, J. (1999). Structure and provision of services in black churches in New Haven, Connecticut. *Cultural Diversity and Ethnic Minority Psychology, 5*(2), 118–133.

Wills, T. A., Yaeger, A. M., and Sandy, J. M. (2003). The buffering effect of religiosity for adolescent substance use. *Psychology of Addictive Behaviors, 17*(1), 24–31.

Yarnold, B. M., and Patterson, V. (1995). Factors correlated with adolescents' use of crack in public schools. *Psychological Reports, 76*, 467–474.

Young, J. L., Griffins, E. H., and Williams, D. R. (2003). The integral role of pastoral counseling by African-American clergy in community mental health. *Psychiatric Services 54*, 688–692.

PART TWO

Case Studies

Alcohol Abuse

"I knew she was drinking too much"

Rev. Roberta Carter learned of Heather Sanders's death early this morning when she read the obituaries in the local newspaper. She was always surprised when members of her church died unexpectedly, and she learned of their passing only from the newspaper. These were typically members who attended infrequently, were middle-aged or elderly, and whose deaths had been related to heart attacks or strokes — acute medical events that had unpredictably ended their lives. But Heather was a different story. She was only 19. Her mother, Jill, was a regular at both Sunday school and church, and Rev. Carter knew Jill well. Heather was halfway through her first year of college at the state university two hours away. Rev. Carter knew she had not been sick. She was shocked by the news of Heather's death and was puzzled as to why she had not heard from Jill. According to the obituary, Heather died two days ago. No mention was made of the cause of death.

Pastoral Assessment

Rev. Carter, called "Bobbi" by almost everyone, immediately phoned Jill. No one answered, and Bobbi left a short message. Jill finally returned the call late the next day. She sounded tired; her tone was flat and devoid of apparent emotion, and her words were few. She did, however, accept Bobbi's offer to stop by the house.

Not until Bobbi got there did she learn from Heather's father, Brad, that Heather died after a party at college. Further gentle inquiry elicited the information that Heather's death had been determined to be a result of alcohol poisoning related to excessive drinking prior to and at the party. Jill and Brad did not believe Heather had ever been much of a drinker, and they had been totally blindsided by the news of her death. They talked with her the week before she died and had no reason to suspect any problems. She was happy, her grades were good, she was on the soccer team, and she had made friends and adjusted well during her first months at school.

Jill said she had not called Bobbi or most of her friends because she did not know how to answer their inevitable questions. "I just don't know what to say."

Bobbie stayed and talked with Heather's parents for over an hour. She knew their grieving had only just begun. The initial shock would wear off, and the reality of the days and years ahead without Heather would be part of their daily lives. Bobbi knew that as their pastor, offering spiritual comfort and guidance was her immediate role and that it would continue to be so in the months ahead. She knew that their church community would also be important in providing spiritual and social support — especially for Jill, who had been very close to her daughter and very involved in the church.

Relevant History Brad and Jill had been married for 26 years. Heather was their first child; their son, Sean, is 17. Brad and Jill drink socially and occasionally, but neither drinks to intoxication or had ever had alcohol or other substance abuse problems.

Heather was an A and B student in high school, was active in school activities, and was a standout on the soccer team. She had grown up in the church, had gone to Sunday school as a child, and had attended services with her mother until she was about 13, when being with friends, playing sports, or sleeping in took precedence over going to church. She had a good relationship with both parents and talked to her mom at least weekly since she had been away at school. She was fairly open in her communication with Jill, often talking not only about what she was doing in classes, but also about her new friends and activities. She even told Jill she was "partying" some with friends from her dorm who were also on the soccer team and was spending time in the "Greek" scene with the older team members. Jill knew she was drinking some-times on weekends and had cautioned Heather to be careful. Heather did not have a car, so Jill was not concerned about her driving under the influence, but Jill asked her to promise not to ride with friends who had been drinking.

Diagnostic Criteria

Alcohol use disorders are categorized in the *Diagnostic and Statistical Manual of Mental Disorders* (DSM) as "alcohol dependence" and "alcohol abuse." Both dependence and abuse are defined as "maladaptive pattern[s] of substance use, leading to clinically significant impairment or distress" with specified criteria occurring at any time during a 12-month period. A diagnosis of *dependence* is based on "tolerance" (a need for increased amounts of the substance for intoxication to occur or lessened effect with the same amount of substance), "withdrawal" symptoms (or using to avoid withdrawal symptoms), an inability to control the use, and/or the substance use having a negative effect on one's social, occupational, or recreational life or on one's physical or psychological health. A diagnosis of *abuse* is appropriate if one's substance use results in "failure to fulfill major role obligations," if one engages in physically hazardous activities while impaired by substances (such as driving a car), has recurrent substance-related legal problems, and/or continues to use "despite having persistent or recurrent social or interpersonal problems caused or exacerbated by the effects of the substance."

Alcohol-induced disorders (as differentiated from alcohol use disorders) include, among many others, "alcohol intoxication." This is the only diagnostic category into which Heather Sanders would have fit. She did not have a pattern of alcohol use that had caused her personal, legal, or academic problems; she did not drive while drunk; she did not experience indications of tolerance to alcohol; and she had never had symptoms of withdrawal. In fact, at the time of her death, she did not meet any of the criteria for alcohol dependence or alcohol abuse.

Binge drinking, which Heather was engaged in on the day she died, is not a DSM category but is a concept commonly understood in the field of alcohol abuse research and treatment. Binge drinking is defined as having five or more drinks per drinking occasion within the past 30 days (Substance Abuse and Mental Health Services Administration, 2002), though some studies define binge drinking for females as four or more drinks per occasion (Jennison, 2004). A survey in 2000 of more than 70,000 people 12 years of age or older in the United States (SAMHSA, 2002) and the survey update including the years of 2002 and 2003 (SAMHSA, 2005) found that almost 20 percent of those ages 12 to 20 were binge drinkers. Binge drinking can lead to alcohol poisoning, a serious and sometimes fatal reaction to heavy episodic alcohol consumption in which the brain is deprived of oxygen; as the body attempts to deal with the excess alcohol and the lack of oxygen to the brain, it can eventually shut down the respiratory and cardiac functions and result in death (SAMHSA, 2000). Alcohol poisoning killed Heather. As her parents learned later from friends who had been with her that day, she had a few beers following soccer practice, then met some friends at a bar, and had a few more drinks before they all went to a fraternity party. At the party she continued to drink because everyone else was, and then for the first time she joined in a drinking game. She eventually passed out, and her friends left her to "sleep it off." She died with an alcohol blood level more than five times higher than the level at which a person is considered to be intoxicated.

Underage alcohol use in general (not just binge drinking) is a significant public health issue. Alcohol is the drug of choice of children and youth, and is used at a higher rate than tobacco or illicit drugs. Forty percent of people who start drinking before age 15 develop alcohol dependence at some time in their lives. Each year approximately 5,000 youth under age 21 die from alcohol-related car accidents, injuries, homicides, and suicides (National Institute on Alcohol Abuse and Alcoholism, 2005b).

Though overall per capita alcohol consumption in the United States is lower today than it was in the 1970s and 1980s, a recent government report shows an increase of 0.9 percent from 2001 to 2002 (Lakins et al., 2004). The economic costs of alcohol abuse in the United States are estimated to have increased from $148 billion in 1992 to $184.6 billion in 1998. Economic costs include such things as alcohol treatment, prevention, research, and training; medical consequences; lost future earnings; crime related costs; social welfare administration; motor vehicle accidents; and fire and other property damages (Harwood, 2000). Underage alcohol consumption has also decreased since the 1970s, but it still continues to be high, as does binge drinking. It occurs even though possession of alcohol by those under 21 years of age is prohibited in all 50 states and consumption is prohibited in most situations in most states. The resultant personal, societal, academic, and medical consequences are often quite substantial — and can include death (Faden and Fay, 2004). For college students aged 18 to 24, drinking alcohol is a factor in an estimated 1,700 student deaths, 599,000 injuries, and 97,000 cases of sexual abuse or date rape annually (Hingson et al., 2005, as cited on *www.collegedrinkingprevention.gov*).

Response to Vignette

Bobbi's response to the Sanders's situation was to be there when they wanted to talk, to offer support, and to help them focus on taking care of business with the university and making other necessary arrangements. Bobbi realized that Jill was embarrassed about the circumstances of Heather's death and that Jill was avoiding neighbors and friends who where calling and stopping by the house. The embarrassment and fear of having to field questions compounded Jill's emotional distress. Bobbi suggested that they plan a response that was honest but not detailed. The Sanders decided to say that Heather's death was totally unexpected. They also prepared a follow-up response to others' well-meaning but unwanted questions; they would say (truthfully) they did not know the details, did not want to discuss it now, and really appreciated the much needed support of their friends at this very difficult time. Bobbi made an announcement to that effect in church that Sunday, and this cued many not to probe for details.

Treatment within the Faith Community

Once the funeral was over, Bobbi continued her regular visits with Jill and Brad. Because of her closer relationship with Bobbi and her history of being connected to the church, Jill was more open to processing her feelings with Bobbi than was Brad. He faded away from their conversations, and soon just Jill and Bobbi talked together. Jill attended church as usual, allowed herself to accept others' expressions of comfort and offers of help, and though her grief was profound, she got through her days.

As Jill learned more about what had happened to Heather, she started to blame herself. "I knew she was drinking some. I should have made her stop! I should have realized the dangers. Why didn't I talk to her more often?"

Many hours of talking with Bobbi helped her understand that she had done the things a good mother does, that Heather had not shown any signs to her parents that she was having any kind of trouble with alcohol. The day she died was the first time she had combined pre-party drinking, playing "chugging" games at a party, and general out of control excessive alcohol consumption. Her friends got drunk that day too, but none realized the extent of Heather's consumption or that her "passing out" would ultimately end with her death.

Jill and Bobbi both began to search the Internet for information on college drinking, and what they found surprised and shocked them. Neither had been aware of the severity of the problem. They found several reliable websites, many resources, and much enlightening information. Jill's embarrassment over the circumstances of Heather's death subsided and was replaced by determination to try to have a positive effect on the problem of underage and college drinking. She talked openly with her son, and they began an ongoing dialog about drinking. She began interacting with other parents in the church on the topic and gave several talks to interested groups. Nine months after she lost her daughter, she organized a group of parents and professionals whose mission was to educate the children, adolescents, and parents of the church about the prevalence and dangers of underage drinking. She had lost Heather, but she was trying to find meaning and purpose for her life despite the tragedy.

A referral to a mental health professional for someone experiencing **Indications** *grief* as a result of the death of a loved one can be made at any point. **for Referral** This is especially recommended if the individual does not have someone supportive, caring, and consistent to talk with over a relatively long period of time. Referrals should be made if a person is having recurrent thoughts of death, is thinking of suicide, is experiencing feelings of worthlessness, is not able to resume relatively normal functioning (such as returning to work, taking care of other family responsibilities) within several months, or is experiencing psychotic symptoms. Bereavement groups can also be helpful as a place to share feelings, hear others' stories, and receive support from those who can likely understand the incredible loss and emotional pain they are experiencing.

Referral to a mental health or substance abuse professional might be made when underage drinking is suspected or confirmed. When working with an adolescent or college student, a trusting relationship might facilitate assessment of a possible drinking problem or a problem drinking behavior (such as binge drinking), education about alcohol use/abuse, and discussion of steps to take to forestall future negative consequences.

A study of adolescents over time from seventh through tenth grade found that religiosity (including factors such as belief in God, praying in times of stress, and relying on religious beliefs) had a buffering effect on substance use (Wills et al., 2003). Therefore, engaging adolescents in activities that strengthen healthy religious beliefs and activities might prove to be beneficial with regard to decreasing the chances of alcohol use.

Treatment by Mental Health Specialist   Bereavement, though not an illness, is a health issue in that it affects one's emotional, social, physical, and psychological well-being (Viney, 2005). Supporting bereaved parents in their grief means recognizing the individuality of each person's experience and needs.

Bereavement counseling includes:

Encouraging the person to talk about the loss;

Helping the person to identify and express feelings (especially anger, guilt, helplessness, sadness);

Assisting the person in making adjustments to live life without the loved one;

Allowing time to grieve;

Helping facilitate understanding of what is normal during grieving (including fears that one is going crazy or will not be able to stand the pain);

Allowing for individualized expressions of grief;

Identifying one's coping styles and behaviors, and assessing for potential harm (such as using drugs or alcohol to numb feelings); and

Recognizing when grief exacerbates other (previous or new) somatic, emotional, or behavioral problems (Worden, 1982).

Traditional models of grief have placed emphasis on the bereaved letting go emotionally of the deceased. Newer models emphasize the value of continuing the bonds with the deceased; this is especially important for grieving parents. Losing a child disrupts the natural order of life and the expectations that parents will die before their children. Maintenance of bonds with the child can occur through conversations that focus on memories of the child, religious acts or other rituals that honor the child (such as praying, planting a memorial tree, lighting candles), writing the child's biography, writing poetry, writing or talking to the child, setting up a memorial fund or other programs, keeping objects that are vivid reminders of the child (such as photos, clothing), or through other ways. Loneliness can become a problem for parents, as others (even spouses and families) often avoid talking with them about their child. Professionals (and bereavement groups) can allow a parent the opportunity to continue a relationship with the child through sharing memories as well as celebrating the life of the deceased child (Davies, 2004).

The normal grieving process varies in the length of time required and in the ways the grief is expressed. A therapist offers a safe place for a bereaved person to express grief, allows for cultural and individual differences in how one processes and copes with grief, offers guidance as one navigates through the bereavement process, and stays alert to symptoms (such as thoughts of suicide) and behaviors (such as substance abuse) that signal a more complicated bereavement or potential problems that need further assessment and treatment. Symptoms such as depressed mood, insomnia, appetite disturbances, or weight loss are common. When symptoms do not abate with counseling, when they continue to worsen over time, or when they are so severe as to be life threatening or to cause functional impairment, then the person must be referred for an evaluation for medication. Therapy is also indicated at this time to uncover and address individual problems and dysfunctional thinking that might be contributing to the development of the symptoms and/or problematic behavior.

Alcohol education programs are common at colleges, but research has found mixed results for the desired effect of decreasing drinking (Donohue et al., 2004; Stamper et al., 2004). Brief interventions with college students who have a history of heavy drinking in high school (Baer et al., 2001), with those who have been required to attend alcohol education or counseling services by their schools because of alcohol-related problems (Barnett et al., 2004), and with college students in general (Miller et al., 2001) have been found to be associated with reductions in alcohol consumption and related problems. Some colleges have established alcohol recovery programs on campus that include residential options such as dorms for former substance abusers who together establish a supportive recovery community (Cole, 2004). A large study in Australia followed individuals from age 14 to 21 and concluded that regular drinking during the teenage years was correlated with alcohol dependency in the young adult years; the researchers caution against viewing alcohol use/abuse as of little concern or just a "rite of passage to adulthood" and recommend early intervention strategies that target adolescents (Bonomo et al., 2004). In addition to taking drinking by young people seriously, another recommendation is that the alcohol industry message that alcohol in moderation is healthful should be balanced with the message of the potential severe harmful effects (Some sobering thoughts, 2004).

Much of the college alcohol abuse research has focused on the prevalence, consequences, and programming to address the problems. One study attempted to identify students' reasons for not drinking and for not playing drinking games. Possible reasons were the students' negative attitudes toward drinking (possibly due to religious views or values), having had bad experiences due to drinking, or having little or no exposure to alcohol or drinking games. Future research in this area might provide valuable information for developing college and youth alcohol abuse prevention programs (Johnson and Cohen, 2004).

Results of a 2002 survey released in 2004 by the Harvard School of Public Health found that 81 percent of administrators of four-year colleges viewed students' alcohol use as a "major problem" or a "problem" on their campus, up from 68 percent in their 1999 College Alcohol Study survey (Wechsler et al., 2004). The 2002 survey of 747 administrators found that all of the schools were engaged in some measures to address the alcohol problems. Actions included banning alcohol on campus (34 percent of the schools surveyed), banning alcohol in residence halls (43 percent), restricting alcohol at school events

(43 percent), providing alcohol education (84 percent provided this for freshman, 72 percent for fraternity/sorority members, and 69 percent for athletes), and other measures. Thirty-five percent of schools surveyed received public/government funding and 21 percent received funding from the alcohol industry for alcohol prevention or education programming. Schools that received industry or public funding were found to be more likely to choose alcohol education and "social norms marketing" as their prevention approach. Social norms marketing (campaigns that attempt to reduce students' alcohol use by correcting misperceptions about the alcohol consumption behavior of their peers) is used in about 75 percent of schools receiving public alcohol education/prevention funding and 70 percent of schools receiving alcohol industry funding. Research has *not* shown social norms marketing to be effective in reducing alcohol use, though other measures, such as limiting access to alcohol, have been shown to have some success. Schools that receive public or alcohol industry funds were also found to be less likely to restrict on-campus alcohol use. The researchers suggest that colleges might want to explore the extent to which funding sources are driving the type of alcohol abuse prevention strategies they provide (Wechsler et al., 2004).

Very brief screening instruments are available to help clinicians assess for alcohol use disorders (NIAAA, 2005a). However when alcohol abuse has been identified as a problem in an individual's life as evidenced by such behaviors as failure in fulfilling work, academic, or family roles, driving when drunk, or experiencing related legal problems, then specific alcohol treatment, including residential treatment, is indicated.

Cross-Cultural Issues

Alcohol use among teenagers is common in many countries. Statistics are difficult to compare due to the differences in the way alcohol use behavior is defined and described and in the way data is categorized (such as using different age group categories). The binge drinking rate of U.S. 12–20-year-olds for the years 2000, 2002, and 2003 is reported to be 19 percent (SAMHSA, 2005). Data from 2000 indicated that those in this same survey who reported past month binge alcohol use varied by race/ethnicity. Underage European-American teenagers reported the highest rate of binge drinking (21.4 percent), with American Indian/Alaska Native next (20.3 percent), followed by Hispanic (17.2 percent), black (10.3 percent), and Asian (7.9 percent). Teenage binge drinking has been reported at 15 percent in Australia, and over 30 percent in Denmark, Ireland, Poland, and the United Kingdom (see Bonomo et al., 2004).

In the United States, the percentage of binge drinkers has been found to increase with age from 0.8 percent at age 12, to 40 percent at age 20. Males are more likely to binge drink than are females. Binge drinking rates for 12–20-year-olds are lower in the Southeast and in West Coast states than in other regions of the country. States in which binge drinking in this age group is estimated to be the highest include Montana, Wyoming, North Dakota, South Dakota, Iowa, Wisconsin, Vermont, and New Hampshire (SAMHSA, 2005). Binge drinking in college students has been shown to correlate with the adult binge drinking rate and with the number of laws that restrict alcohol promotion/sales in the state in which the college is located. States in the lowest quartile of adult binge drinking had a college student binge drinking rate of 36 percent; states in the highest quartile had a rate of 52.7 percent. States with four or more alcohol restriction laws had a college student binge drinking rate of 33.1 percent; states with fewer than four such laws had a rate of 48.3 percent (Nelson et al., 2005).

A study of alcohol use and of heavy episodic drinking in young adults found that in 18–20-year-olds and 21–24-year-olds binge drinking was higher in college students than in noncollege young adults. College students' rates were slightly higher for those living on-campus (54 percent for both age groups) than for those living off-campus (49 percent and 52 percent). College students living with parents had lower rates

(26 percent and 37 percent) in both age groups than those not living at home (Dawson et al., 2004).

Studies have found other factors correlated with college binge drinking including having a history of binge drinking in high school, being an athlete, and living in a fraternity, sorority, or residence hall. These types of living arrangements provide the opportunity for partying and for drinking games (see Boyd et al., 2004, for more information on this research). One study of over 2,000 undergraduate students at a large, public university in the Midwest found that only 25 percent of those living in common residence halls and only 7 percent of those living in fraternities or sororities had never attended a party where drinking games were played (Boyd et al., 2004).

Negative consequences of drinking (such as hangover, vomiting, embarrassment, memory loss, missing classes) were most frequent for those living in fraternities or sororities; negative consequences were more frequent for students living in common residence halls than for those living in substance-free university housing. Of students who reported drinking at all in the past year, only 1 percent had been arrested for driving under the influence — though 35 percent of those living in fraternities or sororities, 27 percent in common residence halls, and 15 percent in substance-free university housing reported having driven a car while under the influence (Boyd et al., 2004).

Resources

Centering Corporation; 7230 Maple Street, Omaha, NE, 68134; (402) 553-1200; *www.centeringcorp.com*; a non-profit organization founded in 1977 and dedicated to providing education and resources for the bereaved; on-line store offers over 300 books, *Grief Digest* magazine, and other related resources.

Centers for Disease Control and Prevention; *www.cdc.gov/alcohol/ index*; an agency of the U.S. Department of Health and Human Services; provides facts and statistics related to alcohol consumption, binge drinking, heavy drinking, alcohol dependence, and underage drinking; the agency's website provides links to other related websites.

The Compassionate Friends (TCF); P.O. Box 3696, Oak Brook, IN, 60522-3696; (811) 969-0010; *www.compassionatefriends.org*; a non-profit, self-help support organization for bereaved parents, grandparents, and siblings; provides chapter locator and links to chapter websites, brochures, grief resources, national magazine, and sibling resources.

National Institute on Alcohol Abuse and Alcoholism; 5635 Fishers Lane, MSC 9304, Bethesda, MD 20892-9304; *www.niaaa.nih.gov*; a part of the National Institutes of Health of the U.S. Department of Health and Human Services. Website provides answers to FAQs as well as pamphlets and brochures in both English and Spanish; information on research studies, conferences, and clinical trials; referral information; and links to related databases.

National Institute on Alcohol Abuse and Alcoholism websites are *www.collegedrinkingprevention.gov* and *www.thecoolspot.gov* (alcohol prevention site for 11–13-year-olds).

Substance Abuse and Mental Health Services Administration; 1 Choke Cherry Road, Room 8-1036, Rockville, MD; *www.samhsa.gov*; the federal government's lead agency for improving the quality and availability of substance abuse prevention, addiction treatment, and mental health services. Comprehensive website provides links to its Center for Substance Abuse Prevention and Center for Substance Abuse Treatment, which provide alcohol-related information, webcasts, programs, publications, resources, news releases, and fact sheets.

SAMHSA National Clearinghouse for Alcohol and Drug Information; *wwwh.ncadi.samhsa.gov*; a comprehensive website offering Tips for Teens, treatment referral resources, a treatment facility locator, webcasts, and government studies and reports.

Bereavement Ministry: A Leader's Resource Manual (Harriett Young, Mystic, CT: Twenty-Third Publications, 1997).

The Bereavement Ministry Program: A Comprehensive Guide for Churches (Jan Nelson and David Aaker, Notre Dame, IN: Ave Maria Press, 1998).

Binge Drinking and Youth Culture: Alternative Perspectives (Malcolm MacLachlan and Caroline Smyth, Dublin: Liffey Press, 2004).

A Broken Heart Still Beats: After Your Child Dies (Anne McCracken and Mary Semel, editors, Center City, MN: Hazelden, 1998).

Choices and Consequences: What to Do When a Teenager Uses Alcohol/Drugs (Dick Schaefer, Center City, MN: Hazelden Foundation, 1998).

Death and Bereavement Across Cultures (Colin Murray Parkes, Pittu Laungani, and Bill Young, editors, London: Routledge, 1997, reprinted 1998 and 2000).

Drugs and Your Kid: How to Tell If Your Child Has a Drug/Alcohol Problem and What to Do about It (Peter D. Rogers and Lea Goldstein, Oakland, CA: New Harbinger, 2002).

Dying to Drink: Confronting Binge Drinking on College Campuses (Henry Wechsler and Bernice Wuethrich, Emmaus, PA: Rodale, 2002).

Finding Hope: When a Child Dies: What Other Cultures Can Teach Us (Sukie Miller with Doris Ober, New York: Fireside/Simon and Schuster, 2002).

The Worst Loss: How Families Heal from the Death of a Child (Barbara D. Rosof, New York: Henry Holt, 1994).

Helpful Books

American Psychiatric Association. (2000). *Diagnostic and statistical manual of mental disorders* (4th ed., text revision). Washington, DC: American Psychiatric Association.

Baer, J. S., Kivlahan, D. R., Blume, A. W., McKnight, P., and Marlatt, G. A. (2001). Brief intervention for heavy-drinking college students:

References

4-year follow-up and natural history. *American Journal of Public Health,* 91, 1310–1316.

Barnett, N. P., Tevyaw, T. O'L., Fromme, K., Borsari, B., Carey, K. B., Corbin, W. R., Colby, S. M., and Monti, P. M. (2004). Brief alcohol interventions with mandated or adjudicated college students. *Alcoholism: Clinical and Experimental Research,* 28, 966–975.

Bonomo, Y. A., Bowes, G., Coffey, C., Carlin, J. B., and Patton, G. C. (2004). Teenage drinking and the onset of alcohol dependence: A cohort study over seven years. *Addiction,* 99, 1520–1528.

Boyd, C. J., McCabe, S. E., and d'Arcy, H. (2004). Collegiate living environments: A predictor of binge drinking, negative consequences, and risk-reducing behaviors. *Journal of Addictions Nursing,* 15, 111–118.

Cole, W. (2004, September 20). Goodbye to the binge: The recovery house. *Time,* 164, 67.

Davies, R. (2004). New understandings of parental grief: Literature review. *Journal of Advanced Nursing,* 46, 506–513.

Dawson, D. A., Grant, B. F., Stinson, F. S., and Chou, P. S. (2004). Another look at heavy episodic drinking and alcohol use disorders among college and noncollege youth. *Journal of Studies on Alcohol,* 65, 477–488.

Donohue, B., Allen, D. N., Maurer, A., Ozols, J., and DeStefano, G. (2004). A controlled evaluation of two prevention programs in reducing alcohol use among college students at low and high risk for alcohol related problems. *Journal of Alcohol and Drug Education,* 48, 13–33.

Faden, V. B., and Fay, M. P. (2004). Trends in drinking among Americans age 18 and younger: 1975–2002. *Alcoholism: Clinical and Experimental Research,* 28, 1388–1395.

Harwood, H. (2000). *Updating estimates of the economic costs of alcohol abuse in the United States: Estimates, update methods, and data.* Report prepared by the Lewin Group for the National Institute on Alcohol Abuse and Alcoholism, National Institutes of Health,

Department of Health and Human Services (NIH Publication No. 98–4327). Rockville, MD: National Institutes of Health. Retrieved September 16, 2005, from *pubs.niaaa.nih.gov/publications/economic-2000/alcoholcost.PDF.*

Hingson, R., Heeren, T., Winter, M., and Wechsler, H. (2005). Magnitude of alcohol-related mortality and morbidity among U.S. college students ages 18–24: Changes from 1998 to 2001. *Annual Review of Public Health*, 26, 259–279.

Jennison, K. M. (2004). The short-term effects and unintended long-term consequences of binge drinking in college: A 10-year follow-up study. *American Journal of Drug and Alcohol Abuse*, 30, 659–684.

Johnson, T. J., and Cohen, E. A. (2004). College students' reasons for not drinking and not playing drinking games. *Substance Use and Misuse*, 39, 1137–1160.

Lakins, N. E., Williams, G. D., Yi, H., and Hilton, M. E., (2004). *Apparent per capita alcohol consumption: National, state, and regional trends, 1977–2003* (National Institute on Alcohol Abuse and Alcoholism Surveillance Report No. 66). Bethesda, MD: National Institutes of Health. Retrieved September 16, 2005, from *www.niaaa.nih.gov/publications/surveillance73/CONS03.htm.*

Miller, E. T., Kilmer, J. R., Kim, E. L., Weingardt, K. R., and Marlatt, G. A. (2001). Alcohol skills training for college students. In P. M. Monti, S. M. Colby, and T. A. O'Leary (Eds.), *Adolescents, alcohol, and substance abuse* (pp. 183–215). New York: Guilford Press.

National Institute on Alcohol Abuse and Alcoholism. (2005a). *Helping patients who drink too much: A clinician's guide.* (NIH Publication No. 05–3769). Rockville, MD: National Institute on Alcohol Abuse and Alcoholism.

National Institute on Alcohol Abuse and Alcoholism. (2005b). *NIAAA initiative on underage drinking.* Retrieved September 16, 2005, at *www.niaaa.nih.gov/AboutNIAAA/NIAAASponsoredPrograms/underage.*

Nelson, T. F., Naimi, T. S., Brewer, R. D., and Wechsler, H. (2005). The state sets the rate: The relationship among state-specific college binge drinking, state binge drinking rates, and selected state alcohol control policies. *American Journal of Public Health, 95,* 441–446.

Some sobering thoughts. (2004, April 8). *Nature, 428,* 587.

Stamper, G. A., Smith, B. H., Gant, R., and Bogle, K. E. (2004). Replicated findings of an evaluation of a brief intervention designed to prevent high-risk drinking among first-year college students: Implications for social norming theory. *Journal of Alcohol and Drug Education, 48,* 53–72.

Substance Abuse and Mental Health Services Administration. *Binge alcohol use among persons aged 12 to 20: 2002 and 2003 update* (The National Household Survey on Drug Abuse Report, August 26, 2005). Retrieved September 30, 2005, from *oas.samhsa.gov/2k5/youthBinge/youthBinge.htm.*

Substance Abuse and Mental Health Services Administration. *Binge drinking among underage persons* (The National Household Survey on Drug Abuse Report, April 11, 2002). Retrieved September 30, 2005, from *www.oas.samhsa.gov/2k2/AlcBinge/AlcBinge.pdf.*

Substance Abuse and Mental Health Services Administration. *Binge drinking in adolescents and college students* (2000 SAMHSA Fact Sheet). Retrieved on September 30, 2005, from *ncadi.samhsa.gov/govpubs/rpo995.*

Viney, A. (2005). Bereavement as a health issue. *Healthcare Counselling and Psychotherapy, 5,* 6–9.

Wechsler, H., Seibring, M., Liu, I., and Ahl, M. (2004). Colleges respond to student binge drinking: Reducing student demand or limiting access. *Journal of American College Health, 52,* 159–168.

Wills, R. A., Yaeger, A. M., and Sandy, J. M. (2003). Buffering effect of religiosity for adolescent substance use. *Psychology of Addictive Behaviors, 17,* 24–31.

Worden, J. W. (1982). *Grief counseling and grief therapy: A handbook for the mental health practitioner.* New York: Springer.

Cocaine

"It made him feel better"

Jason had joined the Marine Corps after two years of college. He went home to his wife, Marilyn, after 12 months in Iraq. Jason's unit had been involved in combat operations, and several of his close buddies did not survive. He seemed perfectly normal when he first returned. However, Jason became more and more irritable over time, and Marilyn realized he was no longer his gregarious self. He was emotionally withdrawn from her, family members, and old friends. When she tried to talk with him about the changes she saw, he became angry, said nothing was wrong, and did not want to talk. Then the horrible nightmares began, keeping him up half the night. Jason had used cocaine occasionally as a recreational drug while in college. Now he began to use the drug in an attempt to self-medicate and to help himself feel better. After Jason went on a weekend binge, Marilyn became desperate and sought out Rev. Templeton for pastoral guidance.

Pastoral Assessment

War is a life-threatening experience that involves witnessing and sometimes engaging in terrifying and gruesome acts of violence. It is normal for human beings to react to war's psychic trauma with profound feelings of fear, anger, grief, repulsion, helplessness, and horror, as well as with emotional numbness and disbelief. Many soldiers are psychologically unable to leave behind the trauma of war when they return home. They struggle with a variety of severe problems that neither they nor their families, friends, or communities understand or know how to address (Weaver et al., 2003).

Combat veterans like Jason may think they are going crazy or there is something wrong with them, since others who were at the same place do not seem to have similar problems. Because thinking about a trauma and feeling endangered is upsetting, those who have experienced combat generally want to avoid all reminders. Survivors may not know what to do to get better. As one might expect, the most important risk factor for veterans' post-traumatic stress disorder (PTSD) is the level of exposure to traumatic events during war (Weaver et al., 2003).

Stress reactions can cause sleep disturbances, irritability, intrusive painful re-experiencing of events, restricted emotional capacity, and impairments of memory and problem-solving capabilities (American Psychiatric Association, 2000). Long-term stress reactions may include depression, chronic anxiety, and the symptoms of PTSD, which include re-experiencing events, as in nightmares or intrusive thoughts; avoidance, such as staying away from situations that remind a person of what happened; restriction in the capacity to experience and express feelings; and a variety of indications of hyperarousal, such as sleep disturbance, an exaggerated startle response, and irritability (American Psychiatric Association, 2000).

A common response is to self-medicate with alcohol or a drug like cocaine to counter distressing feelings and thoughts, as well as guilt over having survived when others died. Perhaps the most perplexing symptom for relatives and friends to understand is psychological numbness: a withdrawal of affection and avoidance of close emotional ties with family members, friends, and colleagues. These responses can cause or exacerbate marital, vocational, or substance abuse problems (Figley, 1989).

Relevant History   Cocaine, a natural alkaloid, was first isolated by a German chemist in 1855. Its use became popular in late nineteenth-century Europe, with many prominent figures praising its therapeutic and recreational value. Cocaine was introduced into clinical use as a local anesthetic in Germany in 1884. About that time Sigmund Freud published a paper, *Über Coca,* in which he lauded its use in the treatment of opiate addiction (Shanti and Lucas, 2003).

By the turn of the twentieth century, the addictive properties of cocaine had become clear to most, and the problem of its abuse began to be recognized. In Western countries, the powdered form of cocaine is a popular recreational drug. In the United States, "crack" cocaine is a cheaper and more powerful, highly addictive form of the drug that is often used in poor urban areas (Gahlinger, 2001). Other slang names for cocaine include: coke, C, snow, flake, lady, blow, jam, happy trails, nose candy, gold dust, and speedball coke. A "speedball" is an especially dangerous combination of cocaine and heroin (Shanti and Lucas, 2003). According to United Nations data, coca production has continued to increase, despite billions of dollars spent to eradicate the problem (Tran, 1998).

Diagnostic Criteria

Cocaine is the most potent stimulant of natural origin. It acts on nerve endings in the brain, increasing the quantity of neurotransmitters such as dopamine at the postsynaptic receptor sites (McCann and Ricaurte, 1999). This buildup of dopamine causes continuous stimulation of receiving neurons, which is associated with the euphoria experienced by abusers. With long-term use, the nerve endings may become depleted of dopamine. This depletion has been theorized to contribute to the depression that develops during withdrawal from cocaine and the subsequent craving for more of the substance (McCann and Ricaurte, 1999). With higher doses and regular use, other neurotransmitter systems (such as serotonin) probably are involved in additional central nervous system toxicity. In studies, animals addicted to cocaine preferred the drug to food, even when it meant they would starve. The addiction is both psychological and physical and can cost thousands of dollars a week to maintain (Gahlinger, 2001).

In its pure form, cocaine is a white crystalline powder. On the street, pure cocaine is frequently adulterated or "cut" with various powdery fillers to increase its volume (Gahlinger, 2001). Cocaine can be snorted, smoked, or injected. When snorted, cocaine powder is inhaled through the nose, where it is absorbed into the bloodstream through the nasal tissues. Regularly snorting the drug can lead to the loss of the sense of smell, nosebleeds, problems swallowing, hoarseness, and a chronically inflamed nose (Gahlinger, 2001). When injected, the abuser uses a needle to release the drug directly into the bloodstream. Smoking involves inhaling cocaine vapor into the lungs, where absorption into the bloodstream is as rapid as by injection. Each of these methods of administration poses great risks to the user.

Crack is the street name given to a form of cocaine that has been processed from powdered cocaine hydrochloride to form a substance that can be smoked (Gahlinger, 2001). The term "crack" refers to the crackling sound heard when the mixture is heated. Crack delivers a strong cocaine experience in small, low-priced packages. It resembles miniature pieces of stone and is often called "rock" on the street. It is heated into a liquid and its fumes inhaled through a pipe in a method called "freebasing," which is especially dangerous because of the high concentrations entering the bloodstream. These high doses can overburden the heart, resulting in sudden death (Gahlinger, 2001).

Users usually feel an initial "rush" — a sense of well-being, having increased energy, and being more alert. This effect quickly wears off, often leaving a user feeling more "down" or depressed than before. This frequently leads an addict to use more cocaine, sometimes just to feel "normal." Over a period of time the amount of cocaine needed and the frequency of use to achieve a "high" has to be increased (American Psychiatric Association, 2000). Feelings of depression can become unremitting.

The use of cocaine in a binge may lead to a state of increasing irritability, restlessness, and paranoia (Gahlinger, 2001). This can progress to paranoid psychosis, in which the user loses touch with reality and experiences auditory hallucinations. Other complications associated with cocaine use include disturbances in heart rhythm and heart attacks, chest pain and respiratory failure, strokes, seizures, headaches, and gastrointestinal complications, such as abdominal pain and nausea (Shanti and Lucas, 2003).

Response to Vignette

After Rev. Templeton listened to Marilyn's expression of concern about her husband, it became clear to him that Jason's drug problem and his PTSD must be addressed. The pastor consulted with a colleague who was a retired military chaplain. They conferred with a psychologist who had expertise in addictions. They decided that the best course of action was a group intervention, involving the pastor, the retired military chaplain, the psychologist, family members, and friends, in which they would help Jason recognize the extent of his drug problem and how his PTSD is related to it. Cocaine users like Jason usually do not know they are out of control. They need feedback through a non-judgmental process to confront the effect of their cocaine use on others. The goal of the intervention is for Jason to accept the reality of his drug addiction and to seek help for that and his PTSD. No group intervention should ever be undertaken without the advice and counsel of a professional experienced in the process.

Treatment within the Faith Community

Unfortunately many soldiers returning from the war in Iraq have not gotten the mental health treatment they need. In July of 2004, the prestigious *New England Journal of Medicine* published a study by researchers at Walter Reed Medical Center. They found that up to 17 percent of combat veterans returning from Iraq had PTSD, but only four in ten of them sought mental health care. The stigma associated with seeking such treatment was the greatest single barrier to obtaining the needed help (Hoge et al., 2004). If the same pattern unfolds that tragically affected Vietnam era veterans and if these PTSD sufferers do not obtain appropriate help, many will become unnecessarily and tragically addicted to drugs or alcohol and commit suicide.

Pastors and churches are in a valuable position to help with these problems. In psychological trauma, an individual's sense of order and continuity of life is shattered and questions of meaning and purpose abound. Studies have shown that religious faith is a primary coping strategy for many people, including recovering combat veterans suffering from psychological trauma (Weaver et al., 2003). In addition to offering the natural social support of community, faith can provide a suffering person with a framework for finding meaning and perspective through a source greater than self, and it can give a sense of control over feelings of helplessness. Research has found that nurturing, non-punitive faith can enhance well-being and facilitate emotional recovery for many traumatized individuals (Weaver et al., 2003).

Clergy are called upon to play a variety of roles as they help trauma survivors move through the healing process. Pastors are accessible and trusted, and through wise counsel they can aid in removing the stigma from mental health care. Clergy are often in long-term relationships with individuals and their families, providing ongoing contacts in which they can observe changes in behavior that can assist in the assessment and treatment of veterans with PTSD. Pastors are also in a position to refer veterans to mental health professionals and support systems available through their faith communities (Weaver et al., 2003).

Indications for Referral   It is important that clergy be knowledgeable about the services provided by the Veterans Administration (VA). The VA medical centers make available a network of more than 100 specialized programs for persons with PTSD, working closely with the centers operated by VA Readjustment Counseling Service (see resources). Each specialized PTSD program offers education, evaluation, and treatment conducted by mental health professionals from a variety of disciplines, such as psychiatry, psychology, social work, and nursing. PTSD clinical teams provide group and one-to-one evaluation, education, counseling, and psychotherapy. Substance use PTSD teams offer outpatient education, evaluation, and counseling for the combined problems of PTSD and substance abuse.

A common issue associated with stress reactions is disturbances within interpersonal relationships. PTSD and other stress-related problems can affect an entire family. Many times family or couple therapy can help a family cope with a veteran's stress-related problems. These types of treatment may include stress-reduction and relaxation techniques that can help all members of the family with the healing process. Therapy might also address the structure of the family and the way that members interact (Figley, 1989).

Treatment by Mental Health Specialist

Cocaine addiction is a significant public health issue. According to national survey data, in 2002 about one in eight admissions for drug and alcohol problems was cocaine addiction related (SAMHSA, 2003). Providing the best possible combination of treatment and services for each individual is critical to successful recovery. Extensive efforts are being made to discover an effective medication to treat cocaine dependency, with some promising advances being made (Dackis, 2004).

Cognitive behavioral therapy has proven to be an effective treatment for many persons (Maude-Griffin et al., 1998). Environment strongly influences an individual's thinking and behavior, so cognitive behavioral therapy teaches new ways of acting and thinking in response to one's surroundings. For example, clients are taught to avoid situations that lead to drug use and to practice skills to say "no" to offers of cocaine. This approach is aimed at helping persons strengthen their commitment to abstinence, deal effectively with urges and risky situations, recognize and change irrational thoughts, manage negative moods, and increase social support (Van Horn et al., 1998).

The 12-step recovery program Cocaine Anonymous has also proven to be effective for many addicts (Wells et al., 1994). The program involves mutual support through group meetings as a way toward recovery from addiction. For many the spiritual component helps members achieve and maintain abstinence. Participants in the groups are introduced to the 12 steps of Cocaine Anonymous and encouraged to work faithfully on the steps of the program one by one. Many recovering persons find it helpful to attend 12-step meetings in addition to their clinic-based group and individual sessions.

Individual therapy is also an important part of treatment, allowing therapists to obtain histories and develop structured treatment plans. In addition, individual therapy gives clients an opportunity to discuss matters that were not covered adequately in groups. Relapse prevention should be a part of any drug treatment program and has proven to help people not return to cocaine use (McKay et al., 1999).

Cross-Cultural Issues The National Survey on Drug Use and Health found in 2003 that almost 35 million Americans aged 12 and older used cocaine in their lifetime and among those, about 8 million used crack (SAMHSA, 2003). Approximately 2.3 million indicated use of cocaine in the past 30 days, and about 600,000 reported using crack in that period of time. Among young adults aged 18 to 25, the rate of abuse was the highest at 15 percent (SAMHSA, 2003). Men have a higher rate of cocaine use than do women. According to the survey, estimated rates of current cocaine users were 2.0 percent for American Indians and Alaskan Natives, 1.6 percent for African-Americans, 0.8 percent for both European-Americans and Hispanics, 0.6 percent for Native Hawaiian and other Pacific Islanders, and 0.2 percent for Asians (SAMHSA, 2003).

Resources American Association of Pastoral Counselors; 9504A Lee Highway, Fairfax, VA 22031; (703) 385-6967; *www.aapc.org*; provides information on qualified pastoral counselors and church-related counseling centers.

American Psychiatric Association; 1000 Wilson Boulevard, Suite 1825, Arlington, VA 22209; (703) 907-7300; *www.psych.org*.

American Psychological Association; 750 First Street, NE, Washington, DC 20002; (800) 374-2721; *www.apa.org*.

Cocaine Anonymous; 3740 Overland Avenue, Suite C, Los Angeles, CA 90034; (310) 559-5833; *www.ca.org*; a fellowship of men and women who share their experiences with each other so that they may help solve their common problem, cocaine addiction.

Hazelden Foundation; Box 176, Center City, MN 55012; (800) 257-7800; *www.hazelden.org.*

International Society for Traumatic Stress Studies; 60 Revere Drive, Suite 500, Northbrook, IL 60062; (847) 480-9028; *www.istss.org.*

National Center for Post-Traumatic Stress Disorder; VA Medical Center, 215 North Main Street, White River Junction, VT 05009; (802) 296-6300; *www.ncptsd.org*; provides information for families, employers, and communities to help support returning veterans in their transition from military to civilian life. Resources and readings are provided, as well as information on preparing for returning veterans, career transition tools, support networks, and more.

National Institute on Drug Abuse; National Institutes of Health, 6001 Executive Boulevard, Bethesda, MD 20852; (301) 443-1124; *www.drugabuse.gov.*

U.S. Department of Veterans Affairs (VA), *www.va.gov.* Provides information on VA programs, veterans' benefits, and VA facilities worldwide. The VA is the parent organization of the National Center for PTSD.

Helpful Books

Clean Start: An Outpatient Program for Initiating Cocaine Recovery (William E. McAuliffe and Jeffrey Albert, New York: Guilford Press, 1992).

Cocaine Addiction: Treatment, Recovery, and Relapse Prevention (Arnold M. Washton, New York: W. W. Norton, 1991).

Counseling Survivors of Traumatic Events: A Handbook for Pastors and Other Helping Professionals (Andrew Weaver, Laura Flannelly, and John Preston, Nashville: Abingdon, 2003).

Crack Cocaine: A Practical Treatment Approach for the Chemically Dependent (Barbara C. Wallace, New York: Brunner-Routledge, 1991).

Post Traumatic Stress Disorder: The Latest Assessment and Treatment Strategies (Marvin Friedman, Kansas City, MO: Compact Clinicians, 2000).

References   American Psychiatric Association. (2000). *Diagnostic and statistical manual of mental disorders* (4th ed., text revision). Washington, DC: American Psychiatric Association.

Dackis, C. A. (2004). Recent advances in the pharmacotherapy of cocaine dependence. *Current Psychiatry Reports, 6*(5), 323–331.

Figley, C. R. (1989). *Helping the traumatized family.* San Francisco: Jossey-Bass.

Gahlinger, P. M. (2001). *Illegal drugs: A complete guide to their history, chemistry, use and abuse.* Ogden, UT: Sagebrush Press.

Hoge, C. W., Castro, C. A., Messer, S. C., McGurk, D., Cotting, D. I., and Koffman, R. L. (2004). Combat duty in Iraq and Afghanistan, mental health problems, and barriers to care. *New England Journal of Medicine, 351*(1), 13–22.

Maude-Griffin, P. M., Hohenstein, J. M., Humfleet, G. L., Reilly, P. M., Tusel, D. J., and Hall, S. M. (1998). Superior efficacy of cognitive-behavioral therapy for crack cocaine abusers: Main and matching effects. *Journal of Consulting and Clinical Psychology, 66*(5), 832–837.

McCann, U. D., and Ricaurte, G. A. (1999). Neuropathology of cocaine abuse. *Current Opinions in Psychiatry, 12*(3), 277–280.

McKay, J. R., Alterman, A. I., Cacciola, J. S., O'Brien, C. P., Koppenhaver, J. M., and Shepard, D. S. (1999). Continuing care for cocaine dependence: Comprehensive 2-year outcomes. *Journal of Consulting and Clinical Psychology, 67*(3), 420–427.

Shanti, C. M., and Lucas, C. E. (2003). Cocaine and the critical care challenge. *Critical Care Medicine, 31*(6), 1851–1859.

Substance Abuse and Mental Health Services Administration (SAMHSA) (2003). *Overview of findings from the 2002 national survey on drug use and health* (Office of Applied Studies, NHSDA Series H-21, DHHS Publication No. SMA 03-3774). Rockville, MD.

Tran, M. (1998). Drugs war is futile exercise. *Guardian Weekly,* June 21.

U.S. Department of Health and Human Services. (2002). *Monitoring the Future Study.* Rockville, MD: National Institute on Drug Abuse.

Van Horn, D. H. A., and Frank, A. F. (1998). Psychotherapy for cocaine addiction. *Psychology of Addictive Behaviors,* 12(1), 47–61.

Weaver, A. J., Flannelly, L. T., and Preston, J. D. (2003). *Counseling survivors of traumatic events: A handbook for pastors and other helping professionals.* Nashville: Abingdon.

Wells, E. A., Peterson, P. L., Gainey, R. R., Hawkins, J. D., and Catalano, R. F. (1994). Outpatient treatment for cocaine abuse: A controlled comparison of relapse prevention and Twelve Step approaches. *American Journal of Drug and Alcohol Abuse,* 20, 1–17.

Compulsive Buying

"She spent everything she made and more"

Jessica is a relatively new member of Pastor John's congregation. She joined the church after she married Steve, a young man whose family has belonged to the congregation for three generations. Jessica is 22 years old and a recent graduate of a nearby university, where she and Steve met. They were married 14 months ago, started their careers in a small town where Steve grew up, and recently bought a home there.

Today she sat in Pastor John's office with her hands in her lap and her head lowered. She glanced up furtively several times and then quickly looked away before making eye contact. Finally she blurted out, "My marriage is over!" and burst into tears. Jessica cried quietly for a minute then looked up at the pastor.

He told her that he was trained and experienced in working with couples and offered to see them together for counseling to help them resolve relationship issues. He asked Jessica to describe the problems they were having. She said they argued "constantly," rarely had fun together anymore, and were having "money problems." Jessica seemed hesitant about scheduling an appointment for them, but did so anyway. Pastor John gave her two questionnaires, one for her and one for Steve to complete prior to their meeting in three days.

To the pastor's surprise, when Jessica arrived for the appointment several days later, she was alone. "The truth is, Pastor, Steve doesn't need to be here. I didn't even tell him I was coming. It's just me. I'm

**Pastoral
Assessment**

the problem." Gentle questioning by Pastor John failed to clarify the problem any further; Jessica seemed embarrassed and was reticent. The pastor asked to see her questionnaire. She had completed it and had obviously put some time and thought into her answers. She indicated many strengths in her marriage including "love," "companionship," "shared interests," "similar values," "our religion," and "friendship." On a checklist of "topics that often result in conflict," she did not check alcohol, drugs, sex, in-laws, work, or any of the other 15 or so items listed. "Finances" *was* marked. Pastor John knew that both Jessica and Steve had good entry-level jobs — she as a math teacher and Steve in the management of the information systems department of the local hospital.

After several probing questions shed no further light on the "finances" problem, John said, "Jessica, please tell me how money is causing problems in your marriage." She gave a big sigh, looked him in the eye, and said, "It's not money that's the problem; it's me. I spend everything I make and more. I shop all the time — at the mall, on the Internet, on the phone. I buy things I don't need. Sometimes I buy things I don't even want!" Jessica continued to pour out her story: "Sometimes I even hide things I buy from Steve. I owe over $18,000 on seven different credit cards. When I'm not shopping, half the time I'm thinking about it. And the worse part is I can't stop! No, wait, the worse part is that Steve is totally fed up with me."

Pastor John thanked Jessica for having the courage to admit her situation to herself and to him. He assured her he would help her confront and resolve the problem.

Relevant History   Jessica grew up as an only child in a home where her interior designer mother and architect father provided well for her materially, but less so emotionally. Her parents worked long hours, frequently late into the evenings and often on weekends. They both had wealthy clients and kept up a certain image — driving high-end cars and wearing expensive clothes. They probably lived above their means, but money was never discussed and certainly was not identified in the family as a problem. When Jessica was younger, an outing with her mother might be a shopping trip where they perused and purchased expensive home furnishings for a client.

Jessica was a bright young woman who had done well in school, but she was shy and introverted and unsure of herself around others. She spent a great deal of time by herself studying, reading, and watching television, and felt more comfortable being alone than in social situations. Jessica had few friends and fewer social activities. She was expected to go to college, which she did, and her education was paid for by her parents. She used a credit card for her books and other purchases at school, and her parents paid the bills. In her junior year she moved from the dorm into an apartment, worked part-time, and met Steve. He was busy with college, his job, and the computer club. They dated exclusively, though they saw each other only two or three times a week. School, work, and Steve provided the parameters of Jessica's life, and she had little other social contact.

Compulsive buying and creating excessive debt is a significant problem among many college students (Mowen and Spears, 1999). Jessica's money problems began on a small scale after she started receiving student credit card applications in the mail. She bought clothes, shoes, and cosmetics, and filled any extra time she had with computer shopping, going to the malls, or looking through the multitude of catalogs that filled her mailbox. The items she bought seemed to hold the promise of beauty, self-confidence, and an exciting social life. The act of buying the items brought only short-lived satisfaction, and so she continually bought — seeking the "high" associated with shopping, buying, spending, and dreaming of wonderful results. Jessica gradually increased her spending and the number of credit cards she had. She asked for more money from her parents, worked more hours, and made minimum payments on multiple credit cards.

After graduation, she received higher spending limits on her card and opened several department store accounts. Even though her parents paid for the wedding, she overspent on "extras" and charged these. Now that she and Steve are homeowners, she has plenty of other reasons for buying. Jessica often purchased things she did not really want or need. She hid these items from Steve when she could and sometimes stored things in her closet or the basement — unopened since purchase. She worried about Steve being home when the mail or delivery truck arrived. Over the past year, though, he could not help but notice the increased shopping and the accumulation of purchases. He frequently expressed his concern and asked her to slow down. Jessica managed for a while to hide the bills, but eventually Steve insisted on seeing them all. He was shocked at the huge amount she owed and was amazed at her ability to creatively juggle so many payments. The interest was very high, and Jessica was making no headway in paying off any of the accounts. Making minimum payments was keeping her one step away from financial ruin, but her continued excessive spending and broken promises to Steve were heading her rapidly toward marital ruin.

Diagnostic Criteria Jessica's behavior is not specifically classified as a psychiatric disorder in the *Diagnostic and Statistical Manual of Mental Disorders*. It is considered by many professionals to fall into a catch-all category of "Disorders of Impulse Control Not Otherwise Specified" (Black, 1996; Kottler, 1999). The behavior is seen by some to be an obsessive-compulsive disorder and by others as an affective-spectrum disorder (Faber, 2004). It has also been termed a "behavioral addiction" (Marks, 1990), and Glatt and Cook (1987) make a case for considering "pathological spending" as a form of psychological dependence similar to drug abuse or pathological gambling. The lack of agreement may be a factor in the problem not being taken as seriously as a psychiatric disorder as it might (Faber, 2004).

The terms used to describe the disorder in the literature include "compulsive buying" (Black, 1996; Faber, 2004; Kwak et al., 2003; Lejoyeux et al., 1997), "pathological spending" (Glatt and Cook, 1987), and "compulsive shopping" (Starace, 2002). An overarching term, "acquisitive desire," is used in relation to hoarding behaviors, greed, and the "neurotic pursuit of possessions" (Kottler, 1999).

As with other impulse control disorders, compulsive buyers experience seemingly uncontrollable urges (in this case, to buy), and tension relief once the urge is acted upon (Monahan et al., 1966). The instant gratification of acting on the urges overshadows any thought of the resultant negative consequences (Kottler, 1999). Psychological disorders related to lack of clarity and meaning in life, self-devaluation, social/relationship deficits, and depressed mood, and whose related behaviors focus on seeking "fleeting pleasures acquired through compelling consumption" (whether in gambling, eating, drugs, sex, and/or buying) manifest themselves in relation to one's culture and environment (Starace, 2002). An individual's experiences, opportunities, social and political environment, and peer and societal pressures shape the expression of the excessive consumption.

Compulsive buying diagnostic criteria for clinical and research use have been developed. The criteria include the elements of *thoughts, behavior,* and *impairment.* According to the criteria, compulsive buying is:

A. Maladaptive preoccupation with buying or shopping, or maladaptive buying or shopping impulses or behavior, as indicated by at least one of the following:

1. Frequent preoccupation with buying or impulses to buy that are experienced as irresistible, intrusive, or senseless.

2. Frequent buying of more than can be afforded, frequent purchase of items that are not needed, or shopping for longer periods of time than intended.

B. The buying preoccupations, impulses, or behaviors cause marked distress, are time-consuming, significantly interfere with social or occupational functioning, or result in financial problems (such as indebtedness or bankruptcy).

C. The excessive buying or shopping behavior does not occur exclusively during periods of hypomania or mania (McElroy et al., 1994, p. 247).

Measurement scales have been developed to aid professionals in the diagnosis of compulsive buying disorder and to rate severity and change in persons who exhibit this behavior (Black et al., 2001; Faber and O'Guinn, 1992; Monahan et al., 1996).

Compulsive buyers often have co-occurring disorders, including depression, anxiety, substance use disorders, trichotillomania (compulsive hair-pulling), and pathological gambling (Black, 1996; Lejoyeux et al., 2002; Lejoyeux et al., 1997); the evidence for co-occurring eating disorders is mixed (Mitchell et al., 2002).

Response to Vignette

Pastor John realized that Jessica's situation required some specialized attention and a comprehensive approach. He offered to help her find a therapist with whom she could explore and resolve the issues related to her excessive buying behavior. Jessica had attempted to make changes on her own for a long time without any sustained success, so she eagerly accepted this offer. She began seeing a therapist who had experience in working with clients with similar problems. She was referred by the therapist to a credit counseling service for education and help in developing a spending and debt repayment plan. Pastor John encouraged Jessica to talk with Steve about her commitment to changing her behavior and her concrete plans to do so. He began seeing Jessica and Steve together to help them learn and use effective communication skills and to assist them in working as a team within the framework of their marriage and spiritual commitments.

The individual therapy, couple's sessions, and credit counseling all proved to be valuable learning experiences for Jessica. She cut up her credit cards, began talking over their joint budget with Steve on a regular basis, and gradually started becoming involved in some church and community activities. Her individual therapy helped her to understand the origins of her behavior and to work on the underlying issues. In the past she had just tried to *stop* the maladaptive behaviors without understanding the roots of the problem or what specific changes in thinking, beliefs, and actions would make ending the behaviors possible.

Jessica came to realize that though her parents loved her and had been good providers, they set the stage for her to engage in compulsive spending. They modeled excessive buying, did not discuss or teach her about finances, and, most importantly, paid little attention to her emotional needs. She did not learn to socialize with family and friends, was not encouraged to develop outside activities or varied interests, and was left alone frequently. Jessica interpreted their actions as indicating that she was not really important, and her rather low self-esteem was a result. She was taught that image was important, and so she attempted as a young adult to buy just the right things to create that image. Jessica did not learn to socialize and relate easily to others, and she later bought things in an attempt to bolster her self-confidence. She had developed little in her life that had any deep meaning, other than her relationship with Steve. Fortunately, though, she did have her marriage, and saving the relationship became the impetus for her to make significant changes in her life.

With the help of her therapist, Jessica was able to identify the underlying distorted ways of thinking that had guided her life so far. Thoughts such as "I'm not very important," "Other people are better looking than I am," "I'll never know how to act around people," and "I'm not good enough" colored her view of herself and the world. Jessica now realized she often interpreted situations in ways that made her life more difficult and that served to lower her self-confidence further and to keep her isolated from others emotionally and socially.

Understanding the roots of her problems and recognizing that she often thought in ways that contributed to them were the first steps in Jessica's major life changes. She now was focused on "catching" herself as often as she could when the old ways of thinking occurred — and then changing the distortions to accurate and productive thoughts. She realized that though her parents had not been emotionally present or expressive, she was "important" and "good enough." Her therapist had her identify her values, and over time Jessica generated a list of values to guide her life. The list included some concepts Jessica had never really thought much about before, including "compassion," "helping others," "total trust within my marriage," and "friends."

Increasing her self-esteem and self-confidence was an ongoing process and was a result of changes in both thinking and actions. At Pastor John's suggestion, Jessica became involved in a women's mission group at the church; she helped cook and serve meals at the homeless shelter once a month and also visited church members who were homebound. These activities expanded Jessica's world, offered her the opportunity to begin acting on some of her newly identified values, provided her a socially non-threatening and structured way to socialize and make friends, and helped her develop respect for herself. And in the process she was helping others. Jessica began to understand what her therapist meant by creating *meaning* in her life. When she understood the *meaninglessness* of a socially isolated life that revolved around shopping, acquiring, and the unsuccessful search for image and acceptance (by herself and others), she was able to curtail her excessive buying. Steve was supportive of her through this process. Jessica's changes, combined with the couple's deeper level of understanding of each other as an outgrowth of their couple's sessions, resulted not only in a fiscal plan for healthier family finances, but also in a stronger marriage.

Treatment within the Faith Community   The pastor recognized Jessica's difficulties as being more than just a behavior problem or lack of responsibility. He facilitated the couple's work on relationship concerns and helped them conceptualize these concerns within the larger context of their spiritual lives. Because Pastor John understood that just telling Jessica to change her behavior would not be successful, he made appropriate referrals. Importantly, though, he encouraged her to become involved in socially active and meaningful outreach with other members of the congregation. These activities decreased her social isolation, positively affected her self-esteem, and helped her shift her focus away from material things and toward spiritual/emotional/social values.

A referral to a mental health professional is necessary when shopping and buying behaviors and/or preoccupations cause impairment as indicated by significant personal or family distress; social, occupational, and/or marital problems; or financial or legal problems (Black, 1996; Lejoyeux et al., 1997). Co-occurring symptoms of other psychological disorders are common with compulsive buying. Mood disorders (especially depression), anxiety, substance abuse, eating disorders, personality disorders, pathological gambling, and trichotillomania have each been identified as co-occurring with compulsive buying, and are all indicators of the need for a referral. **Indications for Referral**

A mental health professional who has experience in treating compulsive buying would be able to work with someone whose behavior causes impairment and/or co-occurs with depressive or anxiety symptoms, personality disorder symptoms, or other impulsive, compulsive, or addictive behaviors. **Treatment by Mental Health Specialist**

Treatment would be multidimensional and comprehensive. As with any therapy, the development of a therapeutic alliance between the professional and a compulsive buyer is important to the outcome (Havens, 2004; Miller, 2004), so helping a person find a therapist with whom he or she can develop a working relationship is a valuable pastoral service.

Kottler and colleagues (2004) outline the following treatment process for persons with any form of "acquisitive desire" disorder, including compulsive shopping. Following their recommendations, a therapist attempts to understand the cultural context of the behavior (such as family/cultural/ethnic traditions, exposure to advertising, peer pressure) and the effects of childhood traumas and emotional or material deprivations. Acquiring possessions might be one's way to self-soothe or an attempt to substitute "things" for the love and attention that was lacking in childhood. A therapist helps a compulsive shopper explore the entire family system to unearth any behaviors of other family members that enable or are otherwise related to the excessive buying. The next step is to identify underlying cognitions one has developed that negatively affect feelings and behavior. Unintended messages resulting from childhood experiences and behaviors modeled by parents often create distorted ways of viewing the world and one's self that in turn lead to maladaptive behaviors. Examining one's belief system and automatic thoughts and then changing any distorted ones to accurate and healthy thoughts is a vital component of therapy. A therapist explores with a compulsive buyer not only the origins of the problem, but also the functions and consequences.

Determining a person's readiness to change and enabling the person to make a *commitment to change* is vital. If a compulsive shopper is not committed to change, then therapy will be unlikely to have a successful outcome. In that case, addressing the barriers to making a commitment is the therapy focus. A therapist guides the compulsive buyer in examining issues related to guilt and shame about the behavior and focuses on identifying and overcoming related skill deficits (such as not being able to interact adequately in social situations). Helping a person find ways to "fill the void" left behind once the time-consuming excessive shopping behavior is eliminated is another step in the therapy process. Creating and finding meaningful activities and a sense of purpose in life can help address this. Finally, a therapist helps the compulsive buyer build support into his or her life for the changes made throughout this process. Support can be family, spouse/partner, 12-step meetings (such as Debtors Anonymous), and/or working with a credit counseling service.

Some research has been conducted on the effects of medication in treating compulsive shopping disorder with the conclusion that it might be effective (Black et al., 1997; Grant, 2003). Obsessive-compulsive disorders are often treated with medications, specifically selective serotonin reuptake inhibitors (SSRIs), and these have been used to treat compulsive buying. Medication might be a useful adjunct to the comprehensive psychotherapy discussed above, but because it does not get to the roots of the problem and because it cannot address needed behavior and cognitive changes, it should not be the primary or only component of treatment (Kottler, 1999).

Cross-Cultural Issues

Although both men and women exhibit compulsive buying behavior, the literature presents the typical profile as female, rather young (under 40), and unmarried (Black, 1996; Black et al., 1997; Lejoyeux et al., 1997). Most of the research on the topic has been published in the past 15 years (Faber, 2004), and so a limited body of related research exists. Therefore, little cross-cultural compulsive buying information is available. One study, however, found that the Diagnostic Screener for Compulsive Buying scale, which was developed by Faber and O'Guinn using U.S. consumers, was not transferable to South Korean consumers (Kwak et al., 2003).

The cultural issue probably most relevant to this disorder is the "consumer culture" of our current society (Kasser and Kanner, 2004). Advertising of an increasing number of products now occurs not only through television, radio, newspapers, and magazines, but it permeates our daily lives. Sports events are sponsored by corporations selling products, Internet sites are full of advertisements, and computer "pop-up" ads are hard to avoid. Even credit card bills come with sales promotions. Buses, benches, and billboards post advertisements. Catalogs clog our mailboxes. New in the print media is the hybrid catalog/magazine that depicts models and celebrities with the latest clothes and goods in a magazine format and gives readers the opportunity to order these items from the pseudo magazine. The overarching corporate advertising message is that happiness is found in material possessions; "internalized corporate culture" occurs when people believe that message and adopt the identity of consumer (Kanner and Soule, 2004).

Multiple research studies (reported in Kasser et al., 2004) have found that people with high materialistic values have more depression, anxiety, narcissism, drug use, and physical symptoms, as well as lower self-esteem, quality of relationships, happiness, and life satisfaction. A high "materialistic value orientation" is also associated with lower social interest (such as desire to make the world a better place or to help others) and with more negative attitudes toward protecting the environment. Humans create the culture and are in turn "created" by it. Cultural pressures to consume and our shared societal view that material possessions equal success, coupled with a person's psychological issues (such as low self-esteem, social skill deficits, history of deprivation, depression), set the stage for maladaptive behaviors such as compulsive buying. The culture of excessive consumption glamorizes image, material possessions, and experiences, sets the stage for people to be emotionally, socially, and environmentally disconnected, and results in decreased life satisfaction.

Psychological research is now beginning to uncover the links between materialism/excessive consumption and individuals' diminished subjective well-being. Suggestions for changes on the personal, professional, family, and societal levels are offered in the literature (Kilbourne, 2004; Kottler, 1999; Levin and Linn, 2004; Winter, 2000, 2004).

Resources   Debtors Anonymous (DA), (781) 453-2743, *www.debtorsanonymous .org,* a non-profit, self-supporting, independent fellowship of individuals who want to stop incurring debt; members meet to share their experiences and to support each other in recovery from "compulsive debting." The website includes a list of DA meetings with contact information and offers books, CDs, videos, tapes, and a newsletter.

National Foundation for Credit Counseling, (800) 388-2227, *www.nfcc .org,* a national nonprofit credit counseling network with more than 1,000 community-based offices around the United States. Its member agencies can be identified by the NFCC seal, which signifies that they meet the high standards for agency accreditation, counselor certification, and policies. Member agencies are often known as the Consumer Credit Counseling Service of the community they represent, and they offer credit counseling, debt reduction services, and education.

Helpful Books

Consuming Passions: Help for Compulsive Shoppers (Ellen Mohr Catalano and Nina Sonenberg, Oakland, CA: New Harbinger, 1993).

I Shop Therefore I Am: Compulsive Buying and the Search for Self (April Lane Benson, editor, Lanham, MD: Jason Aronson Publishers, 2000).

The OCD Workbook: Your Guide to Breaking Free from Obsessive-Compulsive Disorder (Bruce M. Hyman and Cherry Pedrick, Oakland, CA: New Harbinger, 1999).

Overcoming Overspending: A Winning Plan for Spenders and Their Partners (Olivia Mellan, New York: Walker and Company, 1995).

Psychology and Consumer Culture: The Struggle for a Good Life in a Materialistic World (Tim Kasser and Allen D. Kanner, editors, Washington, DC: American Psychological Association, 2004).

References

American Psychiatric Association. (2000). *Diagnostic and statistical manual of mental disorders* (4th ed., text revision). Washington, DC: American Psychiatric Association.

Black, D. W. (1996). Compulsive buying: A review. *Journal of Clinical Psychiatry, 57,* 50–55.

Black, D. W., Monahan, P., and Gabel, J. (1997). Fluvoxamine in the treatment of compulsive buying. *Journal of Clinical Psychiatry, 58,* 159–163.

Black, D. W., Monahan, P., Schlosser, S., and Repertinger, S. (2001). Compulsive buying severity: An analysis of compulsive buying scale results in 44 subjects. *Journal of Nervous and Mental Disease,* 189, 123–126.

Faber, R. J. (2004). Self-control and compulsive buying. In T. Kasser and A. D. Kanner (Eds.), *Psychology and consumer culture: The struggle for a good life in a materialistic world* (pp. 169–187). Washington, DC: American Psychological Association.

Faber, R. J., and O'Guinn, T. C. (1992). A clinical screener for compulsive buying. *Journal of Consumer Research*, 19, 459–469.

Glatt, M. M., and Cook, C. C. H. (1987). Pathological spending as a form of psychological dependence. *British Journal of Addiction*, 82, 1257–1258.

Grant, J. E. (2003). Three cases of compulsive buying treated with naltrexone. *International Journal of Psychiatry in Clinical Practice*, 7, 223–225.

Havens, L. (2004). The best kept secret: How to form an effective alliance. *Harvard Review of Psychiatry*, 12, 56–72.

Kanner, A. D., and Soule, R. G. (2004). Globalization, corporate culture, and freedom. In T. Kasser and A. D. Kanner (Eds.), *Psychology and consumer culture: The struggle for a good life in a materialistic world*. Washington, DC: American Psychological Association.

Kasser, T., and Kanner, A. D. (Eds.) (2004). *Psychology and consumer culture: The struggle for a good life in a materialistic world* (pp. 169–187). Washington, DC: American Psychological Association.

Kasser, T., Ryan, R. M., Couchman, C. E., and Sheldon, K. M. (2004). Materialistic values: Their causes and consequences. In T. Kasser and A. D. Kanner (Eds.), *Psychology and consumer culture: The struggle for a good life in a materialistic world* (pp. 11–28). Washington, DC: American Psychological Association.

Kilbourne, J. (2004). "The more you subtract, the more you add": Cutting girls down to size. In T. Kasser and A. D. Kanner (Eds.), *Psychology and consumer culture: The struggle for a good life in a materialistic world* (pp. 251–270). Washington, DC: American Psychological Association.

Kottler, J. A. (1999). *Exploring and treating acquisitive desire: Living in the material world*. Thousand Oaks, CA: Sage Publications.

Kottler, J., Montgomery, M., and Shepard, D. (2004). Acquisitive desire: Assessment and treatment. In T. Kasser and A. D. Kanner (Eds.), *Psychology and consumer culture: The struggle for a good life in a materialistic world* (pp. 149–168). Washington, DC: American Psychological Association.

Kwak, H., Zinkhan, G. M., and Crask, M. R. (2003). Diagnostic screener for compulsive buying: Applications to the USA and South Korea. *Journal of Consumer Affairs*, 37, 161–169.

Lejoyeux, M., Arbaretaz, M., McLoughlin, M., and Ades, J. (2002). Impulse control disorder and depression. *Journal of Nervous and Mental Disease*, 190, 310–314.

Lejoyeux, M., Tassain, V., Solomon, J., and Ades, J. (1997). Study of compulsive buying in depressed patients. *Journal of Clinical Psychiatry*, 58, 169–173.

Levin, D. E., and Linn, S. (2004). The commercialization of childhood: Understanding the problem and finding solutions. In T. Kasser and A. D. Kanner (Eds.), *Psychology and consumer culture: The struggle for a good life in a materialistic world* (pp. 213–232). Washington, DC: American Psychological Association.

Marks, I. (1990). Behavioural (non-chemical) addictions. *British Journal of Addiction*, 85, 1389–1394.

McElroy, S. L., Keck, P. E., Pope, H. G., Smith, J. M., and Strakowski, S. M. (1994). Compulsive buying: A report of 20 cases. *Journal of Clinical Psychiatry*, 55, 242–248.

Miller, M. C. (2004). Questions and answers: How important is the therapeutic alliance for the outcome of psychotherapy, and how should it affect a patient's choice of therapist? *Harvard Mental Health Letter*, 21, 7–10.

Mitchell, J. E., Redlin, J., Wonderlich, S., Crosby, R., Faber, R., Miltenberger, R., Smyth, J., Stickney, M., Gosnell, B., Burgard, M., and Lancaster, K. (2002). The relationship between compulsive buying and eating disorders. *International Journal of Eating Disorders, 32,* 107–111.

Monahan, P., Black, D. W., and Gabel, J. (1996). Reliability and validity of a scale to measure change in persons with compulsive buying. *Psychiatric Research, 64,* 59–67.

Mowen, J. C., and Spears, N. (1999). Understanding compulsive buying among college students: A hierarchical approach. *Journal of Consumer Psychology, 8,* 404–430.

Starace, G. (2002). New "normalities," new "madnesses." *British Journal of Psychotherapy, 19,* 21–31.

Winter, D. D. (2000). Some big ideas for some big problems. *American Psychologist, 55,* 516–522.

Winter, D. D. (2004). Shopping for sustainability: Psychological solutions to overconsumption. In T. Kasser and A. D. Kanner (Eds.), *Psychology and consumer culture: The struggle for a good life in a materialistic world* (pp. 69–87). Washington, DC: American Psychological Association.

Computers—Excessive Internet Use

"She lost herself in the virtual reality"

Sam Miller sat alone in church again this Sunday. He and his wife, Linda, used to attend church together, but for the last few months she had often chosen to stay at home. David, the pastor, had noticed and several times had asked Sam about Linda. His inquiries were always met with a slight shrug and an excuse of some kind, but with little detail. Today, however, was different. Sam approached David after the service and asked if he would make a visit to their home in the near future. The pastor agreed, and they set up a time.

When David arrived the next Saturday morning, Sam greeted him at the door. They sat down with a cup of coffee, but Linda did not appear until Sam went into their office ten minutes later to ask her to join them. She apologized and said she had been working on the computer.

After some small talk, Sam told David that he was concerned about Linda spending so much time on the computer. The pastor laughed and said he too probably spent too much time on Internet searches, getting derailed on tangents instead of sticking to the research he had originally intended. Sam did not laugh along with David but instead said that his wife's Internet use was a huge problem as far as he was concerned. Not only was she "surfing the net" on Sunday mornings instead of attending church, she was spending most of her evenings and weekends on the computer, too.

They talked some more and David eventually told Linda he missed seeing her at church; he encouraged her to start attending again. She agreed she would try.

Three weeks later, David still had not seen Linda back at church, and he asked Sam how things were going at home. Sam told him that she seemed to be totally immersed in the Internet when she was not at work. He said that Linda was spending time on the Internet at the expense of their marriage, friendships, social life, church involvement, and every other aspect of her life. She no longer worked out at the gym and rarely even went to the grocery store. "She's addicted to the Internet, and it's ruining both of our lives!"

Pastoral Assessment   After his last talk with Sam, David realized that he had initially underestimated the problem. He decided to do some research on the topic of Internet use. Ironically, he did his investigation online. He located journal articles that he read and also ordered several books from an online bookseller. After educating himself on the topic, he understood that the Millers were facing a complex and possibly serious problem.

David asked to meet with them again. This time he did not make light of the situation, but asked direct and pointed questions about Linda's Internet use and about the consequences. She was evasive at first. Then Sam detailed the negative effects of her spending so much time and being engrossed in chat rooms, reading and writing e-mail, browsing stores and auction websites, following political happenings, playing games, and just "surfing the 'net." He said they no longer ate meals together or went out to dinner or the movies; she had given up exercise, friends, church, baking, volunteer work, and her garden, and had even postponed their vacation indefinitely. He went on to say that she was not getting enough sleep because she often stayed up until 1:00 a.m. on the computer and then had to get up for work before 6:00 a.m. "We basically have no life together and no Internet-free life at all!"

Linda is 47 years old and has been married to Sam for 12 years. **Relevant** They have no children. Her father died suddenly two years ago of a **History** heart attack, and her mother died six months ago after a three-year battle with breast cancer. Linda was an only child. She had always been emotionally and geographically close to her parents. Even after she and Sam married, they continued frequent contact — having meals together weekly, talking on the phone almost daily, and even going on vacations together a few times.

After her father's death, Linda checked in with her mother regularly, took her to medical appointments, and toward the end of her life spent hours with her while she was hospitalized. The stress associated with her role as caregiver, coupled with the pain of knowing her mother was dying, took an emotional toll on Linda. In actuality, long before she became engrossed in the Internet, she had started to curtail many of her social activities out of necessity.

Losing both her parents within a two-year period was very difficult for Linda. Though on the outside she appeared to be doing well, on the inside she felt empty, sad, and lonely. She worried at times about who would take care of her when she got old or became ill. She missed her parents and had not been able to reestablish the previous rhythm of her life.

Linda discovered that she could distract herself from sad or frightening thoughts and from her pain by losing herself in the virtual reality of the Internet. Sam was unaware that she was even spending time at work surfing the net. She knew this was risky since it was against company policy to do other than work-related computer activities on the job. Linda began spending more time at home online, and the more time she spent, the more diversions she found. She searched medical information websites, belonged to an online bereavement support group, e-mailed and "chatted" with people she had never met, browsed the websites of her favorite stores, and even started playing games — everything from solitaire to interactive ones in which she took on a virtual identity. She realized she was spending too much time doing this. Initially it helped her avoid her pain. Then it became fun and as such reinforced her continuing the behavior. Then it became her life.

Diagnostic Criteria   No diagnostic criteria for excessive Internet use are included in the American Psychiatric Association's *Diagnostic and Statistical Manual of Mental Disorders* (DSM). The term "addiction" is often applied to behaviors, not just to ingestion of substances, but it is not used in the DSM. What is generally meant by "addiction" most closely resembles the DSM category of "dependence." Internet "addiction" might also fall under the category of impulse control problems (Treuer et al., 2001). A variety of terms in addition to *addiction* are used in the relatively new area of research examining Internet use, including *Internet behavior dependence* (Hall and Parsons, 2001) and *excessive, problematic, and maladaptive Internet use* (Beard, 2002; Caplan, 2002). In 1996 Young developed an eight-item screening instrument for "addictive Internet use," which modified the DSM criteria for pathological gambling. The questions address feelings of preoccupation with the Internet; unsuccessful efforts to decrease time spent on the Internet; related negative moods; staying online longer than offline; risking significant relationship, career, or educational opportunities; lying to others about one's Internet use; and using the Internet as an escape from problems or emotional pain. Exhibiting five of the eight items is considered to differentiate between normal and pathological Internet use (Young, 1999).

Negative consequences of excessive Internet use can include family and marriage problems, academic difficulties, and occupational problems (Young, 1999). Depression and obsessive-compulsive disorder symptoms (Beard, 2002) in some people result in, and/or are exacerbated by, excessive Internet use. Regardless of the term used or the diagnoses given, when Internet use becomes problematic, treatment is indicated.

Linda initially wanted to avoid even talking about her Internet use and did not want to address the situation as a *problem*. She recognized that she was isolating herself and thinking more about her virtual world than real life, but rationalized that no real harm resulted. Linda had convinced herself that since she was not visiting pornography websites, engaging in "cybersex," having online intimate chats with men, gambling, or spending much, her behavior was harmless. **Response to Vignette**

When Sam expressed his distress to David, he opened the door to discussion and examination of the negative effects of Linda's behavior. When he got her attention long enough to have a real conversation, Sam, with David's assistance, was able to convey his feelings and fears to Linda. When confronted with the facts, Linda began to become aware of the consequences both to her and to her marriage. She agreed to work on changing her behavior, but said she did not know how.

David's research on the topic of excessive Internet use enabled him to help Linda. He knew that simply encouraging her to stop the problematic behavior was not enough. He now understood something about the complexity of such a situation, and so he decided to help Linda find a counselor who was familiar with treating this type of problem. In addition, he talked with her about some of her Internet activities and discovered that she belonged to an online bereavement support group. He introduced her to a colleague of his, another pastor, who led a weekly group for grieving persons. Linda agreed to attend, and after several weeks, found that she was able to be supported and to provide support to *real* people. The bereavement group became a lifeline connecting her to the world. She started to attend church again, and the opportunity to reconnect with her spiritual self brought her comfort. **Treatment within the Faith Community**

Linda's Internet use, though problematic, is relatively mild compared to some excessive Internet users. Discussions and examples abound in the literature of people who have experienced extremely negative consequences of pathological Internet use (Griffiths, 2000; Schneider, 2000; **Indications for Referral**

Young 1996). Financial, family, marital, physical, and mental health can be severely affected. When Internet use is such that it negatively affects one's life and a person is not able to decrease his or her use to a reasonable level, outside help is needed. In addition to the previously listed factors, other indications for referral to a mental health specialist include depressed mood, anxiety, social isolation, loneliness, marital problems, and obsessive-compulsive behaviors. These might be causally related to or result from excessive Internet use.

Treatment by Mental Health Specialist   The research on excessive use of the Internet and on related symptoms and treatment is new and inconclusive. More research is needed to identify when treatment interventions might be useful so that Internet users can take advantage of the Internet's many benefits while avoiding its potentially harmful effects (Song et al., 2004). Any mental health professional treating a person with excessive Internet use as part of a presenting problem needs to be informed by the literature that is available. Online and telephone counseling is offered through the Center for Online and Internet Addiction (see Resources), but can be expensive (Oreilly, 2000); this might be an alternative for individuals who do not have access to in-person therapy because of geographical remoteness or other reasons.

Though the term "addiction" is often applied to excessive Internet use, the treating professional should be aware that one is not addicted to the Internet per se, but is reinforced by the information available online, the experience of interactivity/competence/power resulting from directing the computer activity, and/or the continual novelty of the evolving technology (Shaffer et al., 2000).

A treating therapist can use a brief screening instrument to assess the extent and effects of Internet use (Young, 1999). A client can also be assessed for depressive symptoms, low self-esteem, anxiety, family or marriage problems, academic or work difficulties, maladaptive thoughts, compulsive behaviors, substance abuse, pathological gambling, and other problems of impulse control. Family issues that might be a factor in the development of excessive computer or Internet use, and/or that might have resulted from the excessive use should be addressed in therapy (Oravec, 2000; Young, 1999). A person's motivation for change can also be assessed and motivational enhancement therapy used as indicated (Orzack, 1999).

Problematic Internet use is viewed as a result of maladaptive ways of thinking coupled with behaviors that intensify or maintain the excessive Internet use, plus an underlying psychological problem (such as depressed mood, social anxiety, substance dependence) and a social context (such as social isolation, divorce) that sets the stage (Davis, 2001).

Cognitive behavior therapy is a recommended treatment for excessive Internet use (Davis, 2001; Hall and Parsons, 2001; Orzack, 1999). A client and therapist identify maladaptive thoughts (such as "Nobody loves me [off-line]," "I'm never going to be happy [off-line]," "I'm a failure [but nobody online knows that]"), identify triggers to such thinking, and then the client is taught and encouraged to challenge and restructure the distorted thoughts. The new ways of thinking are accurate and functional for the person's life.

Young (1999) recommends several techniques for treatment:

1. Practice the opposite — disrupt routines and develop new patterns of daily behavior;

2. External stoppers — prompters to log off (alarm clock signals for places one is scheduled to be);

3. Setting goals — developing a structured plan for decreasing computer use;

4. Abstinence — from specific problematic Internet sites or computer applications (chat rooms, games, auctions, pornography sites);

5. Reminder cards — written cards to remind one of goals, negative and positive effects of excessive Internet use;

6. Personal inventory — creating a list of activities one has significantly reduced or eliminated from his or her life to allow the person to recognize that he or she can return to real-life experiences;

7. Support group — online or through an addiction recovery hospital or other treatment facility;

8. Family therapy — to educate, reduce blame, improve communication, and encourage family assistance in the client's changes.

Linda was depressed following the illnesses and deaths of her parents. Her therapist helped her identify the thoughts that were contributing to the unresolved bereavement (such as "I'm alone now," "I'm old and don't have much of my life left either"). They discussed these and other maladaptive ways of thinking, and Linda was able to successfully challenge and restructure her thoughts. She benefited from the bereavement support group and realized that her sadness and thoughts were not unusual. She was able to restructure them to more adaptive ones (such as "I miss my parents, but I have a great husband"; "I'm getting older, but I am in good health and have lots of life left in me"). She took a personal inventory and began remembering the activities that had been important to her. As a result, she began slowly adding these activities back into her life.

She found that setting goals around her computer use was helpful. She did not want to completely quit using it as that would be unrealistic, but she stopped going to chat rooms altogether. She later decided to eliminate using the online support group, since her real-life group was more satisfying. And she gave up time-wasting games completely. Linda found that her behavior and cognitive changes reaped rewards. Her initial reentry into the world was with the assistance of her therapist, who was understanding, supportive, and helpful. The therapeutic alliance that developed allowed Linda to begin looking outward, past her virtual world. She was able to reconnect with Sam, with her church, and with an old friend. Her mood improved as a result of her changes and that made making further change easier. After less than three months of therapy, Linda had curtailed her excessive Internet use and re-created her life.

Cross-Cultural Issues

The anonymity of the Internet makes determining who uses it excessively (to the detriment of their lives and the lives of those around them) very difficult. In addition, methodological problems make it hard to draw meaningful conclusions both within a study and between studies. These problems include: inconsistency among studies regarding the conceptualization and definition of the problem, inconsistency in criteria and assessment tests used in the studies, and the fact that subjects in the studies are not representative of the general population since they are often recruited through the Internet and/or are college students (Kaltiala-Heino et al., 2004). Online surveys and research are limited in their usefulness because the subjects are self-selected Internet users who respond to such surveys.

One study (Young and Rodgers, 1998) examined the relationship between depression and excessive Internet use. The subjects were recruited online from electronic support groups and from people who searched for keywords "Internet" or "addiction" on search engines. The sample included 130 male and 129 female "addicted [Internet] users"; mean age was 31 for the males and 33 for the females. This study suggested that non-tech or high-tech white-collar workers were more likely to use the Internet excessively than were blue-collar workers. This might be due to wider computer and Internet accessibility for white-collar workers on the job and at home.

The Center for Online and Internet Addiction (*www.netaddiction .com*, 2005) reported that almost 6 percent of over 17,000 respondents in an online survey met its criteria for compulsive Internet use. Its research showed a mean age of 23 for males and 43 for females. Non-tech white-collar workers represented 39 percent of the respondents, 8 percent were high-tech white-collar workers, 11 percent were blue-collar workers, and 42 percent indicated no occupation (but identified homemaker, disabled, retired, students).

A review of the literature showed the results of several studies conducted in countries other than the United States. A self-selected sample of 7,878 males and 5,710 females accessed through an Internet portal site in Korea found that 3.5 percent were "Internet addicts" (IA), and 21.67 percent were "possible Internet addicts" (PA), based on the subjects' scores on an eight-item scale developed by Kimberly Young and adapted from the diagnostic criteria for pathological gambling. The IA group reported the highest rates of loneliness, depressed mood, and compulsivity when compared to the other PA or non-addict groups (Whang, Lee, and Chang, 2003).

In a study of 700 high school students in Taiwan (ages 16–17), two questionnaires were used to assess "Internet addiction" — Young's scale, and the Internet Addiction Scale for High School Students in Taiwan. Sixty students were identified as "Internet addicts." In-depth interviews were conducted with ten of these (eight males and two females). The students spent more than 20 hours per week on the Internet. The study concluded that these young people used the Internet as their "principal information source and a place of relief" (Tsai and Lin, 2003).

Forty-one undergraduate students in Stockholm, Sweden (20 female, 21 male, average age 21), participated in a study. Frequent Internet use was found to be correlated with greater loneliness and higher "deviant values" and with poorer work-leisure balance and selected measures of emotional intelligence, such as being able to identify emotions in facial expressions and in social situations (Engelberg and Sjoberg, 2004).

A representative sample of 7,292 12–18-year-olds in Finland was surveyed through the mail. The study found that 1.7 percent of the boys and 1.4 percent of the girls met the criteria for "Internet addiction." These statistics are lower than in many other studies, but the authors conclude that even so, further studies on possible psychological and social harm should be conducted since Internet use is increasing rapidly and, presumably, excessive use will continue to increase, too (Kaltiala-Heino et al., 2004).

The computer and the Internet are ubiquitous in the lives of many, if not most, people in the developed world, and as such, the door is open for anyone to develop a pattern of excessive and pathological use. Problematic use can occur in any age, socioeconomic, racial, or educational group. Both men and women are vulnerable to the problem.

Resources

Center for Internet Studies, *www.virtual-addiction.com*, the website of clinical psychologist David Greenfield, provides information, education, and resources on e-behavior and Internet addiction. Articles are available on this site including "Ten Steps to Reclaim Real-Time Living." Annotated links to related resources are provided.

Center for Online and Internet Addiction, *www.netaddiction.com*, is an online training institute and recovery center founded in 1995 and specializing in Internet addiction and related online mental health conditions. Online support groups are provided, along with on-line counseling for individuals, couples, and families whose lives have been negatively affected by "sexual addiction, virtual adultery, compulsive e-auctioning" or stock trading. Continuing education training is offered for health care providers; links are provided to resources and research articles; downloadable brochures are available.

Computer Addiction Services, a treatment program of McLean Hospital; 115 Mill Street, Belmont, MA 02478; (617) 855-2908; *www.computeraddiction.com*; founded by Maressa Hecht Orzack, a clinical psychologist at Harvard University. The website lists physical and psychological symptoms of computer addiction. It has a section of questions and answers with Dr. Orzack and links to related articles.

Helpful Books

Caught in the Net: How to Recognize the Signs of Internet Addiction — And a Winning Strategy for Recovery (Kimberly Young, New York: John Wiley and Sons, 1998).

Cybersex Exposed: Simple Fantasy or Obsession? (Jennifer Schneider and Robert Weiss, Center City, MN: Hazelden, 2001).

The Psychology of the Internet (Patricia Wallace, New York: Cambridge University Press, 2001).

Virtual Addiction: Help for Netheads, Cyberfreaks, and Those Who Love Them (David N. Greenfield, Oakland, CA: New Harbinger, 1999).

References American Psychiatric Association. (2000). *Diagnostic and statistical manual of mental disorders* (4th ed., text revision). Washington, DC: American Psychiatric Association.

Beard, K. W. (2002). Internet addiction: Current status and implications for employees. *Journal of Employment Counseling, 39,* 2–11.

Caplan, S. E. (2002). Problematic Internet use and psychosocial well-being: Development of a theory-based cognitive-behavioral measurement instrument. *Computers in Human Behavior, 18,* 553–575.

Davis, R. A. (2001). A cognitive-behavioral model of pathological Internet use. *Computers in Human Behavior, 17,* 187–195.

Engelberg, E., and Sjoberg, L. (2004). Internet use, social skills, and adjustment. *CyberPsychology and Behavior, 7,* 41–47.

Griffiths, M. (2000). Does Internet and computer "addiction" exist? Some case study evidence. *CyberPsychology and Behavior, 3,* 211–218.

Hall, A. S., and Parsons, J. (2001). Internet addiction: College student case study using best practices in cognitive behavior therapy. *Journal of Mental Health Counseling, 23,* 312–328.

Kaltiala-Heino, R., Lintonen, T., and Rimpela, A. (2004). Internet addiction? Potentially problematic use of the Internet in a population of 12–18-year-old adolescents. *Addiction Research and Theory, 12,* 89–96.

Oravec, J. A. (2000). Internet and computer technology hazards: Perspectives for family counselling. *British Journal of Guidance and Counselling, 28,* 309–324.

Oreilly, M. (2000). Internet addicts can get online help. *Canadian Medical Association Journal, 163,* 199.

Orzack, H. M. (1999). Computer addiction: Is it real or virtual? *Harvard Mental Health Letter*, 15(7), 17

Schneider, J. P. (2000). A qualitative study of cybersex participants: Gender differences, recovery issues, and implications for therapists. *Sexual Addiction and Compulsivity*, 7, 249–278.

Shaffer, H. J., Hall, M. N., and Bilt, J. V. (2000). "Computer addiction": A critical consideration. *American Journal of Orthopsychiatry*, 70, 162–168.

Song, I., Larose, R., Eastin, M. S., and Lin, C. A. (2004). Internet gratifications and Internet addiction: On the uses and abuses of new media. *CyberPsychology and Behavior*, 7, 384–394.

Treuer, T., Fabian, Z., and Furedi, J. (2001). Internet addiction associated with features of impulse control disorder: Is it a real psychiatric disorder? [Letter to Editor]. *Journal of Affective Disorders*, 66, 283.

Tsai, C., and Lin, S. S. J. (2003). Internet addiction of adolescents in Taiwan: An interview study. *CyberPsychology and Behavior*, 6, 649–652.

Whang, L. S., Lee, S., and Chang, G. (2003). Internet over-users' psychological profiles: A behavior sampling analysis on Internet addiction. *CyberPsychology and Behavior*, 6, 143–150.

Young, K. (1996). Psychology of computer use: Addictive use of the Internet: A case that breaks the stereotype. *Psychological Reports*, 79, 899–902. Retrieved January 30, 2005, from *www.netaddiction.com/articles/stereotype.htm*.

Young, K. (1999). Internet addiction: Symptoms, evaluation, and treatment. In L. VandeCreek and T. Jackson (Eds.), *Innovation in clinical practice: A source book* (pp. 19–31). Sarasota, FL: Professional Resource Press. Retrieved January 30, 2005, from *www.netaddiction.com/articles/symptoms.htm*.

Young, K. S., and Rodgers, R. C. (1998). The relationship between depression and Internet addiction. *CyberPsychology and Behavior*, 1. Retrieved January 30, 2005, from *www.netaddiction.com/articles/cyberpsychology.htm*.

Ecstasy—MDMA

"Jangling keys sounded danceable"

Rev. Linda Norris had been the campus minister for six years when Amy came to her office with her story. She had gone to a club to dance with a friend and was frightened at what happened. She had taken Ecstasy for the first time, and it scared her.

She told the campus minister that about thirty minutes after taking the drug, her heart went into overdrive and she felt hot and sticky while her mouth became dry. Even the sound of jangling keys sounded danceable and people she did not know became huggable. The lights in the room seemed brighter, and colors were more intense. The next day she felt depressed, anxious, tired, dehydrated, and frightened. Prior to this experience she had little familiarity with illicit drugs, although she drank alcohol in moderation.

Pastoral Assessment

Rev. Norris had counseled several students who had tried Ecstasy. It was a popular drug on campus, and more than one student had ended up in the emergency room from taking too much. Many problem users' encounters with Ecstasy are similar to those found with the use of amphetamines and cocaine.

The clergywoman knew it was important to share accurate information with Amy and to help her educate herself about the effects and risks of Ecstasy. Rev. Norris told Amy that she was aware of an increased use of "club drugs" (also known as "designer drugs"), such as Ecstasy (McDowell, 1999). The terms "club drugs" or "designer drugs" refer to a wide range of synthetic compounds produced in secret labs. They are used on college campuses and in bars, dance clubs, or all-night dance parties featuring computer-generated, high volume, pulsating music (colloquially termed "raves" or "trances"). Like other club drugs, Ecstasy is illicitly made, adding to its danger the risk of impurity and contamination from unknown substances. An analysis of confiscated Ecstasy revealed a wide range of added ingredients, including methamphetamine and cocaine (Sherlock et al., 1999).

Relevant History   MDMA (Ecstasy) was an unplanned by-product of a chemical synthesis discovered in 1912. It was patented in Germany by the pharmaceutical firm Merck in 1914 (McDowell, 1999). In the 1950s it was tested by the U.S. government as a truth serum as part of the CIA's and the army's chemical warfare investigations. In the middle 1970s, it began to be used as an adjunct to psychotherapy by psychiatrists and therapists who were familiar with the field of psychedelic psychotherapy (McDowell, 1999). In the early 1980s, the drug began to be used non-medically under the name Ecstasy. Soon afterwards its use rapidly spread outside the United States as well. In 1985 MDMA was prohibited by the Drug Enforcement Administration when it was given the same status as heroin and LSD (McDowell, 1999). It is currently estimated to be the most popular club drug in Europe and the United States (SAMHSA, 2003).

Diagnostic Criteria   Ecstasy, or MDMA (3,4-methylenedioxymethamphetamine), is a psychoactive drug, chemically similar to the stimulant methamphetamine and the hallucinogen mescaline. In its pure form, it is a white crystalline powder. It is usually seen in capsule form, in pressed pills, or as loose powder. It is most commonly swallowed or snorted, although it can be smoked or injected (Cohen, 1998).

Street names for MDMA include Ecstasy, adam, XTC, hug, beans, and love drug (Cohen, 1998). MDMA is a relatively simple compound to synthesize and the profit margins are high. Street value for MDMA tablets can reach as high as $40 per tablet, while the cost of production is rarely more than 25 cents per pill (Shannon, 2000). In 2002, an estimated 676,000 people in the United States aged 12 and older used MDMA (SAMHSA, 2003). Ecstasy exerts its primary effects in the brain on neurons that use the chemical serotonin to communicate with other neurons. The serotonin system plays an important role in regulating mood, aggression, sexual activity, sleep, and sensitivity to pain (McDowell, 1999).

Ecstasy's effects can last up to 24 hours. To extend the effects many users will "bump" the drug, taking a second dose when the effects of the initial dose begin to fade. The drug produces side effects, and some (such as confusion, depression, sleep problems, anxiety, and paranoia) can occur weeks after it is taken (McDowell, 1999). MDMA seems to be unique in that it builds up empathy to a high degree and creates a strong emotional link with others present. It is these effects that made MDMA popular as a recreational drug.

Recent data collected by the National Institute on Drug Abuse (NIDA) show that approximately 11 percent of high school seniors have experimented with MDMA, a figure that has doubled over the past five years (National Institute on Drug Abuse, 2001). A survey of over 14,000 college students attending 119 four-year U.S. universities indicated that MDMA use rose from 2.8 percent in 1997 to 4.7 percent in 1999, an increase of 69 percent (Strote et al., 2002).

Research conducted by NIDA indicates that use of club drugs, particularly in conjunction with alcohol, can result in significant complications, including death. This is a concern, particularly in light of data indicating that the use of club drugs is increasing. This trend may be due in part to the erroneous and potentially lethal misperception that these drugs are safe and harmless (McDowell, 1999).

The effects of long-term MDMA use are just beginning to undergo scientific analysis. Tissue samples taken from monkeys suggest that Ecstasy can damage brain cells that release the chemical serotonin for several years (Hatzidimitriou et al., 1999). Ongoing research aims to further clarify the effects of Ecstasy on the brain (SAMHSA, 2003).

Response to Vignette

Rev. Norris had three meetings with Amy. She gave Amy several articles to read about Ecstasy and other common club drugs like Ketamine, Gamma-hydroxybutryate (GHB), LSD, and Rohypnol (see "Other Club Drugs" on page 83). Amy had been frightened by her experience, and she was keen to learn more about the club drugs and their effects. She became motivated to inform her friends about the drugs and started a class at the campus church on drug awareness and prevention.

Treatment within the Faith Community

There is solid scientific evidence that individuals involved in nurturing, non-punitive religion are less likely than the general population to abuse illicit substances like MDMA (Yacoubian, 2003), take part in the excessive use of addictive substances, and suffer the adverse effects of dependence (Larson et al., 1998). Religious practice and strength of religion in the family are inversely associated with anti-social behavior in young people, including fewer drug and alcohol problems (Weaver et al., 1999). In developing prevention efforts that target young people, faith communities need to develop strategies to counter the increasing use and widespread availability of the club drugs such as Ecstasy.

In 1991 the University of Texas Medical Center surveyed 75 percent of the clergy in Galveston, Texas, and found that no congregation in the community had a specific ministry to addicted persons or their families (Turner, 1995). The majority of those contacted expressed interest in learning more about addiction and increasing their counseling skills. The Medical Center developed a successful monthly training program for pastors responding to alcohol and drug addiction, which has increased congregational and clergy involvement in the issue. This type of program can help coordinate efforts to decrease the use of illicit substances through education and awareness.

There is indication of increasing numbers of visits to emergency rooms for MDMA-related complications (Drug Abuse Warning Network, 2000). MDMA can suppress the need to eat, drink, or sleep, enabling users to endure two- to three-day parties sometimes resulting in severe dehydration or exhaustion. MDMA can cause other adverse effects including nausea, hallucinations, chills, sweating, increases in body temperature, tremors, involuntary teeth clenching, muscle cramping, and blurred vision (McDowell, 1999). MDMA users also report aftereffects of anxiety, paranoia, and depression. An MDMA overdose is characterized by high blood pressure, faintness, panic attacks, and, in more severe cases, loss of consciousness, seizures, and a drastic rise in body temperature. MDMA overdoses can be fatal, as they may result in heart failure or extreme heat stroke (McDowell, 1999). **Indications for Referral**

It is important to prepare a list of professional and community resources for addiction problems before being faced with an immediate need to assist someone. Develop appropriate plans of action with mental health colleagues before an emergency occurs.

Rev. Norris was a certified member of the Association of Professional Chaplains. She had four years of graduate training in theology along with over 1,600 hours of clinical supervision to prepare her for her work as a campus minister and certified chaplain. The clinical pastoral education (CPE) training she received helped her integrate her counseling skills with her theological education to prepare her to intervene effectively with students like Amy. Clergy with CPE training report greater confidence as counselors than clergy without the preparation (Orthner, 1986). **Treatment by Mental Health Specialist**

African-American students have considerably lower rates of Ecstasy use than either Hispanic or European-American students. For example, past year use among African-American 12th graders was 1.3 percent, compared to 7.6 percent for European-American 12th graders and 10.6 percent for Hispanic 12th graders (U.S. Department of Health **Cross-Cultural Issues** and Human Services, 2000). Non-Ecstasy users were significantly more likely than Ecstasy users to believe that religion was a very important part of their life. Compared to non-Ecstasy users, those who used MDMA were significantly more likely to approve of the regular use of most illegal drugs, including marijuana and cocaine (Yacoubian, 2003).

Resources   American Academy of Addiction Psychiatry; 1010 Vermont Avenue, NW, Suite 710, Washington, DC 20005; (202) 393-4484; *www.aaap.org*.

American Academy of Child and Adolescent Psychiatry has a website with free information on teen problems, including drug abuse at *www.aacap.org*.

American Council for Drug Education; 164 West 74th Street, New York, NY 10023; (800) 883-DRUG; *www.acde.org*.

American Society of Addiction Medicine (ASAM); 4601 North Park Avenue, Upper Arcade, Suite 101, Chevy Chase, MD 20815; (301) 656-3920; a medical society dedicated to educating physicians and improving the treatment of individuals suffering from alcoholism and other addictions.

Hazelden Foundation; Box 176, Center City, MN 55012; (800) 257-7810; *www.hazelden.org*.

National Center on Addiction and Substance Abuse at Columbia University; 152 West 57th Street, 12th floor, New York, NY 10019; (212) 841-5200; *www.casacolumbia.org*.

National Clearinghouse for Alcohol and Drug Information; P.O. Box 2345, Rockville, MD 20847; (800) 729-6686; *www.health.org*; provides free useful materials about the many aspects of adolescent alcohol and drug abuse treatment and prevention. Several of these publications are designed for the faith community.

National Institute on Drug Abuse; National Institutes of Health, 6001 Executive Boulevard, Room 5213, Bethesda, MD 20892-9561; (301) 443-1124; *www.drugabuse.gov/ResearchReports/MDMA*.

Ecstasy: The Complete Guide: A Comprehensive Look at the Risks and Benefits of MDMA (Julie Holland, Rochester, VT: Park Street Press, 2001). **Helpful Books**

Illegal Drugs: A Complete Guide to Their History, Chemistry, Use and Abuse (Paul M. Gahlinger, Ogen, UT: Sagebrush Press, 2001).

The Love Drug: Marching to the Beat of Ecstasy (R. S. Cohen, Binghamton, NY: Haworth Medical Press, 1998).

LSD: Still With Us After All These Years: Based on the National Institute of Drug Abuse Studies on the Resurgence of Contemporary LSD Use (Leigh A. Henderson and William J. Glass, New York, Jossey-Bass, 1998).

Cohen, R. S. (1998). *The love drug: Marching to the beat of ecstasy.* Binghamton, NY: Haworth Medical Press. **References**

Drug Abuse Warning Network (DAWN). (2000). *Club drugs.* Rockville, MD: U.S. Department of Health and Human Services, Substance Abuse and Mental Health Services Administration.

Hatzidimitriou, G., McCann, U. D., and Ricaurte, G. A. (1999). Altered serotonin innervation patterns in the forebrain of monkeys treated with 3,4-methylenedioxymethamphetamine seven years previously: Factors influencing abnormal recovery. *Journal of Neuroscience, 19,* 5096–5107.

Larson, D. B., Swyers, J. P., and McCullough, M. E. (1998). *Scientific research on spirituality and religion.* Rockville, MD: National Institute for Healthcare Research.

McDowell, D. M. (1999). MDMA, ketamine, GHB, and the "club drug" scene. In M. Galaner and H. D. Kleber (Eds.), *The American Psychiatric Press textbook of substance abuse treatment* (2nd ed., pp. 295–308). Washington, DC: American Psychiatric Press.

National Institute on Drug Abuse. (2001). *Advance report — Proceedings of the Community Epidemiology Work Group.* Rockville, MD: U.S. Department of Health and Human Services.

Orthner, D. K. (1986). *Pastoral counseling: Caring and caregivers in the United Methodist Church*. Nashville: General Board of Higher Education and Ministry of The United Methodist Church.

Shannon, M. (2000). Methylenedioxymethamphetamine (MDMA, "Ecstasy"). *Pediatric Emergency Care, 16*, 377–380.

Sherlock, K., Wolff, K., Hay, A. W., and Conner, M. (1999). Analysis of illicit Ecstasy tablets: Implications for clinical management in the accident and emergency department. *Journal of Accident and Emergency Medicine, 16*, 194–197.

Strote, J., Lee, J. E., and Wechsler, H. (2002). Increasing MDMA use among college students: Results of a national survey. *Journal of Adolescent Health, 30*, 64–72.

Substance Abuse and Mental Health Services Administration (SAMHSA) (2003). *Overview of findings from the 2002 national survey on drug use and health* (Office of Applied Studies, NHSDA Series H-21, DHHS Publication No. SMA 03-3774). Rockville, MD.

Turner, N. H. (1995). Bridging the gap: Addressing alcohol and drug addiction from a community health perspective. *American Journal of Public Health, 85*(6), 870–871.

Weaver, A. J., Preston, J. D., and Jerome, L. W. (1999). *Counseling troubled teens and their families: A handbook for pastors and youth workers*. Nashville: Abingdon Press.

U.S. Department of Health and Human Services. (2000). *Monitoring the Future Study*. Rockville, MD: National Institute on Drug Abuse.

Yacoubian, G. S. (2003). U.S. correlates of ecstasy use among high school seniors surveyed through Monitoring the Future. *Drugs: Education, Prevention and Policy, 10*(1), 65–72.

OTHER CLUB DRUGS

Ketamine (slang or street names: K, ket, special K, vitamin K, vit K, kit kat, keller, kelly's day, Green, Blind squid, Cat valium, Purple, special la coke, super acid, and super C).

Ketamine, or ketamine hydrochloride, is a rapid-acting anesthetic that has been approved for both human and animal use in medical settings since 1970. About 90 percent of the ketamine legally sold today is intended for veterinary use.

Ketamine gained popularity for abuse in the 1980s, when it was realized that large doses cause reactions similar to those associated with use of phencyclidine (PCP, or "Angel Dust"), such as dissociative states, numbness, loss of coordination, sense of invulnerability, muscle rigidity, aggressive/violent behavior, slurred or blocked speech, exaggerated sense of strength, and a blank stare. It is being used by an increasing number of young people as a "club drug" and is often distributed at "raves" and parties.

Ketamine is produced in liquid form or as a white powder that is often snorted or smoked with marijuana or tobacco. The more potent ways of using it are by injection, intramuscularly or intravenously. Low doses (25–100 mg) produce psychedelic effects quickly. At higher doses, ketamine can cause delirium, amnesia, impaired motor function, high blood pressure, depression, and potentially fatal respiratory problems. Long-term effects include tolerance and possible physical and/or psychological dependence.

Gamma-hydroxybutryate, GHB (slang or street names: liquid X, g-juice, grievous bodily harm, G, liquid ecstasy, georgia home boy).

OTHER CLUB DRUGS (continued)

GHB can be produced in clear liquid, white powder, tablet, or capsule forms, and it is often used in combination with alcohol, adding to its danger. GHB was once sold in health food stores to bodybuilders because it was believed to help stimulate muscle growth, but it was pulled off the market in 1990 because of its negative side effects. GHB's intoxicating effects begin 10 to 20 minutes after the drug is taken. The effects typically last up to four hours, depending on the dosage. At lower doses, GHB can relieve anxiety and produce relaxation; however, as the dose increases, the sedative effects become severe. Overdose of GHB can occur swiftly, and the signs are similar to those of other sedatives: drowsiness, nausea, vomiting, headache, loss of consciousness, loss of reflexes, impaired breathing, and ultimately death.

GHB has been increasingly involved in poisonings, overdoses, "date rapes," and fatalities. The drug is used predominantly by youth, often when they attend nightclubs and raves. It is inexpensive and easy to obtain, making it a frighteningly powerful weapon in the hands of potential rapists.

Rohypnol (slang or street names: circles, forget me drug, forget me pill, getting roached, la rocha, lunch money drug, mexican valium, pingus, r-2, reynolds, rib, roach-2, roapies, robutal, roofies, rope, rophies, row-shay, ruffles, wolfies).

Rohypnol is a brand name for flunitrazepam (a benzodiazepine), a very potent tranquilizer similar to Valium (diazepam), but many times stronger. Rohypnol can be ingested orally, snorted, or injected. It is often taken with alcohol. The drug produces a sedative effect, amnesia, muscle relaxation, and a slowing of

OTHER CLUB DRUGS (continued)

psychomotor responses. It can mentally and physically paralyze an individual.

Much of the concern surrounding Rohypnol is its abuse as a "date rape" drug. Sedation occurs 20 to 30 minutes after administration and lasts for several hours. The drug is often distributed on the street in its original "bubble packaging," which adds an air of legitimacy and makes it appear to be legal.

Lysergic Acid Diethylamide, LSD (slang or street names: acid, alice, blotters, sugar cubes, yellow sunshine, white lighting).

LSD is a hallucinogen manufactured from lysergic acid, which is found in ergot, a fungus that grows on several grains. Prior to 1967, LSD was available legally in the United States. It was popularized in the early 1960s by people like Harvard professor Timothy Leary, who encouraged American youth to "turn on, tune in, and drop out." After 1967, underground LSD use continued, supported by a black market and demand for the drug. LSD is sold on the street in tablets, capsules, and, occasionally, liquid form. It is odorless, colorless, and has a slightly bitter taste. Often LSD is added to absorbent paper, such as blotter paper, and divided into small decorated squares, with each square representing one dose.

LSD is a powerful drug that can dramatically affect an individual's sensations and feelings. Although most LSD drug experiences include both pleasant and unpleasant aspects, the effects of the drug are unpredictable and depend on the amount taken, the user's personality, mood, and expectations, and the surroundings in which the drug is used. On an LSD "trip," which may last up to 12 hours, a person may feel several different emotions at

OTHER CLUB DRUGS (continued)

once and experience dramatic and rapid emotional swings. In large doses, LSD produces delusions and visual hallucinations.

Colors, smells, sounds, and other sensations seem highly intensified. In some cases, sensory perceptions may blend in a phenomenon known as synesthesia, in which a person seems to hear or feel colors and see sounds. Some LSD users experience severe, terrifying thoughts and feelings, fear of losing control, fear of insanity and death, and despair while using LSD. These changes can be frightening and can cause panic and fatal accidents. Some users experience flashbacks, a recurrence of certain aspects of a person's drug experience without the user having taken the drug weeks, months, or even years afterward.

Excessive Exercise

"She averaged 20 hours a week exercising"

Emily was the picture of youthful health — twenty-one, tall, and athletic. She was inconsistent in her attendance at church, so Pastor Dave Coles did not know her well. After church last Sunday, though, she asked if she could stop by and talk with him. They arranged a time, and now she sat in his office.

With no hesitation she began to explain why she was there. "My life is out of balance, and I want to change that. I want to lead a more spiritual life. That's really important to me, but I don't know how to do it. I'm so busy, but I feel like I'm just spinning my wheels and not really accomplishing anything."

Pastor Coles asked Emily to tell him about her life, and he settled in to listen. At times he asked a question to elicit a fuller picture. Emily told him she was a student at the state university and was studying to become a dietician. She was also working 15 hours a week at a health food store near campus. She said her free time was taken up with exercising at the gym, running, and leading a couple of aerobics classes at the community center. Though she had attended church as a youngster, she gradually drifted away from it when she was in high school. Now it rarely fit into her busy schedule. "I miss being connected to a church, but making that commitment sure hasn't been a priority for me!"

Pastor Coles and Emily met several more times to chat briefly. She always came carrying her workout bag, sometimes having just completed a workout and sometimes on her way to the gym or to teach an aerobics

Pastoral Assessment

class. Pastor Coles noticed this pattern and also noticed that her left ankle was wrapped with a support bandage and that she was limping. He began asking direct questions regarding her exercise and was surprised to learn that Emily averaged 20 hours a week either weight training, teaching exercise classes, or running. She had continued this routine in the past week despite a twisted ankle. When he questioned her about the reasons and effects of this much exercise, Emily laughed and said, "I guess I am addicted to exercise, but I like it! And at least I'm not starving myself like I used to." She told Pastor Coles that she used to severely restrict her food intake, but that she had been treated several years ago for an eating disorder and no longer had the problem. The pastor knew a little about eating disorders and wondered if some of the same causes and issues associated with Emily's past eating disorder might apply to her excessive exercising. During their talk, Emily confirmed his suspicion that control, body image, and self-esteem issues were indeed factors in her now controlled eating disorder. She was intrigued by his hypothesis that similarities between the two (food restricting and excessive exercise) might exist, but insisted that exercise was healthful while the eating disorder had been a *threat* to her health.

Relevant History Emily was raised in a stable and loving family in which she was nurtured and was emotionally supported. When she was eight years old she was sexually molested by an adult male neighbor. As a result she began isolating herself in her room and she started wetting the bed at night. Her parents noticed these changes in her behavior, and when they talked with her she told them what had happened. They were supportive and attempted to reassure her that she was safe and that she had done nothing wrong. They reported the incident to the police, but no legal action ever occurred. The man moved out of town and no follow-up was done by the family or the police.

Emily began restricting her food intake when she was about 12. She began avoiding family meals to conceal her food restricting behavior; eventually she became very thin. Her parents took her to the family doctor, who was able to diagnose the eating disorder after ruling out other causes for her weight loss. She began seeing a woman therapist and worked through some of the issues related to the sexual abuse, including low self-esteem and feelings of anxiety and guilt. She subsequently resumed normal eating. She did not require hospitalization for the disorder because she was treated early and her condition was not severe. Emily did well socially and academically in high school, played on the soccer team, and participated in other sports whenever she could.

Diagnostic Criteria

Behaviors such as drug and alcohol abuse and cigarette smoking are labeled "addictions" due to observable and measurable physiological responses that result from the abuse and/or from attempted or actual cessation of the use of these substances. Other behaviors are often labeled as "addictions" (such as pathological gambling, self-starvation or anorexia nervosa), although these behaviors do not parallel substance use disorders since no external substance is introduced into the body. Researchers have attempted to find a relationship between endorphins (neurochemicals that create what is often referred to as a "runner's high") produced by exercise and a physical dependence on the endorphins, but no proof of this has been found, and no clear, widely accepted conclusions related to this theory have been made (see Cox and Orford, 2004). Excessive exercising, like gambling and restricting food intake, is conceptualized by some as a type of addiction and by others as a form of obsessive-compulsive disorder. Cox and Orford (2004) caution against pathologizing high-frequency exercise behavior, and instead advocate viewing it within the larger social, environmental, gender, and cultural contexts of the individual.

Criteria for "exercise dependence" were proposed (Veale, 1987), but have not been included in the *Diagnostic and Statistical Manual of Mental Disorders* (2000). Adams and colleagues (2003) modified the criteria that are based on the concepts of tolerance, withdrawal, and compulsive behavior. Their criteria for exercise dependence are: A maladaptive pattern of exercise behavior, leading to clinically significant impairment or distress as manifested by three or more of the following, occurring at any time in the same 12-month period:

1. Tolerance to exercise, as defined by either of the following:

    ◆ A need for markedly increased amounts (frequency, duration and/or intensity) to achieve the same effect.

    ◆ Markedly diminished effect with continued exercise of the same frequency, duration, and/or intensity.

2. Withdrawal from exercise, as manifested by either of the following:

    ◆ Characteristic withdrawal symptoms, such as anxiety, depression, irritability, tension, guilt, frustration, lethargy, malaise in the absence of exercise.

    ◆ Exercise occurring to relieve or avoid withdrawal symptoms.

3. Exercise often occurring in longer duration or more frequently than intended.

4. Exercising even when the individual does not "feel like it."

5. A great deal of time spent exercising.

6. Exercise continued despite a physical or psychological problem that is likely to have been caused or exacerbated by the exercise (such as a recurrent injury).

7. Important social, occupational, or recreational activities given up or made secondary to exercise.

8. Continued exercise despite persistent or recurrent social or interpersonal problems caused or exacerbated by the exercise (such as amount of time exercising).

9. Recurrent exercise resulting in a failure to fulfill major role obligations at work, school, or home.

The nature of excessive exercising as a disorder, and whether it should even be classified as a disorder, remains in question. The lack of consistency in the literature regarding the definition and the terms used to describe the behavior reflects this lack of agreement and clarity. "Excessive exercise" (Davis and Claridge, 1998) is also referred to as "exercise dependence" (Hausenblas and Fallon, 2002; Ogden et al., 1997), "high frequency exercise" (Cox and Orford, 2004), "obligatory exercise" (Steffen and Brehm, 1999), "exercise addiction," "compulsive exercising," morbid exercising," "athletic neurosis" (as cited in Adams et al., 2003; Basson, 2001; Hausenblas and Downs, 2002; Ogden et al., 1997), and "anorexia athletica" (*Anorexia Nervosa and Related Eating Disorders*, 2005) among other terms.

A variety of instruments and scales have been developed to assess exercise behavior. These include the Exercise Dependence Questionnaire (Ogden et al., 1997), Commitment to Exercise Scale (Davis et al., 1993, as cited in Steffen and Brehm, 1999), Obligatory Exercise Questionnaire (Pasman and Thompson, 1988, as cited in Steffen and Brehm, 1999), Exercise Beliefs Questionnaire (Loumidis and Wells, 1998, as cited in Loumidis and Wells, 2001), Exercise Dependence Scale (Hausenblas and Downs, 2002), and the Exercise Commitment Survey (Garman et al., 2004). Researchers use these to further evaluate and understand exercise behavior, and clinicians can use them to evaluate clients' behaviors and to measure change over time. Assessing exercise frequency alone is insufficient for determining whether an individual has a problem related to excessive exercising. One's reasons for exercise and one's overall life functioning are what is clinically important.

When exercise activity dominates one's life and becomes more important than family, friends, and work, when it excludes other recreational activities, and/or when it is engaged in despite physical pain, injury, or illness, then it can be seen as rising to the level of "exercise abuse" (Davis, 2000) or "addiction" (Basson, 2001). Excessive exercising is often related to an eating disorder (Davis et al., 1998; Davis, Katzman, and Kirsh, 1999; Loumidis and Wells, 2001), and so the identification of excessive exercise should be closely linked to evaluation for eating disorders, which are often severe and can be life threatening.

Response to Vignette

Pastor Coles recognized that Emily was indeed correct in saying that her life was out of balance. He knew that her exercise-related activities dominated her life to the exclusion of many social and religious activities. Because she mentioned having a history of an eating disorder, Pastor Coles considered the possibility that she might have other related issues, possibly as a result of childhood neglect, abuse, or other trauma. Emily reported that she had had a positive experience and a successful outcome in her past therapy, and so Pastor Coles encouraged her to check in with the therapist to see if her current time-consuming and excessive exercise behavior might be related to old issues.

Treatment within the Faith Community

Pastor Coles also invited her to begin to take a more active role in the church. Though she declined to be a leader in Sunday services as some members were, she did agree to be a greeter for two Sundays the following month. Because of the pastor's offer to personally introduce her to some church members involved in an ongoing service project to prepare and serve meals to the homeless, she made a commitment to him to do this two hours a week. Emily had reached out to Pastor Coles for help in developing a more religiously oriented life; the church in turn offered her these activities that would provide the opportunity for social connection as well as for spiritual growth.

Indications for Referral

Excessive exercise is often associated with an eating disorder, and so any counselor should be alert for symptoms of anorexia nervosa and bulimia nervosa. Signs and symptoms to watch for include refusal to maintain even a minimally normal body weight; intense fear of gaining weight or becoming fat; distorted body image (such as believing one is fat when quite the opposite is true); absence of menses; binge eating; self-induced vomiting; misuse of laxatives, diuretics, or enemas;

fasting to prevent weight gain; and/or excessive exercise. Eating disorders can result in physical changes and damage, such as hormonal and related menstrual disturbances; osteoporosis; infertility; hot/cold sensitivity; dry skin; brittle hair; soft downy hair growth on the face, arms, or back; dehydration; electrolyte imbalance; cardiac arrhythmias; kidney problems; damage to teeth (from stomach acid as a result of vomiting); and sometimes even death (Abraham and Llewellyn-Jones, 1995). Due to the potential severity of the effects of eating disorders, a referral to a mental health professional should be made any time eating disorders are suspected. Excessive exercise can be a red flag for an eating disorder.

Significant symptoms of anxiety or depression are indications for referral, as are obsessive-compulsive behaviors (such as repetitive hand washing or checking) that cause the person marked distress (Steketee, 1999). Low self-esteem and personality traits such as perfectionism and rigidity might also signal that the person could benefit from some counseling or therapy.

Treatment by Mental Health Specialist

Exercise is generally seen as quite positive and adaptive and is often reasonably recommended by counselors as an adjunct to therapy or just as a positive addition to one's life. Any mental health professional should be cautious about recommending or supporting exercise activities before first assessing the client's exercise beliefs, eating disorder–related beliefs, and coping styles (Loumidis and Wells, 2001).

A mental health specialist who is knowledgeable about eating disorders will be aware of the sometimes associated problems of excessive exercise. She or he will assess the severity of the problems and the individual's related experiences and other factors, and will work with the client to address the identified issues. These issues might include other obsessive compulsive behaviors; research has suggested that obsessive-compulsive cleaning rituals, eating disorders, and a history of sexual abuse are all linked (Lockwood et al., 2004). Other problems might include low self-esteem; feelings of helplessness, guilt, lack of control;

anxiety and/or depression; sleep disturbances; and/or resultant medical conditions. Psychological, interpersonal, social, and biological factors should be explored in an attempt to determine the genesis of the disorder(s) and to inform treatment. A dysfunctional family or other dysfunctional personal relationships, a history of being teased as a child about body weight or size, a history of sexual or physical abuse, social pressures to be thin (National Eating Disorder Association, 2005), media images that promote thinness (Nemours Foundation, 2005), a history of rape, the death of a loved one, participating in sports or activities that emphasize low weight such as gymnastics or dance, or even giving birth (APA Help Center of the American Psychological Association, 2005) can be causes of eating disorders and associated excessive exercise. Once the pattern of excessive exercising is established, it can be self-perpetuating.

Thorough assessment of the exercise behavior can be accomplished through the use of one of the exercise scales (see Diagnostic Criteria section) and/or through a structured interview. Exploring the underlying reasons for the behavior allows treatment to focus on education, and on the cognitive and behavior changes necessary for a successful outcome.

Adams and colleagues (2003) recommend a cognitive behavioral therapeutic approach to working with individuals who meet the criteria for exercise dependence. Core strategies for treatment include:

- Identifying and interrupting the behavior through individual therapy; and
- Assisting persons in:
  - understanding the health benefits of moderation
  - developing a self-management plan
  - understanding their psychological defenses and coping patterns
  - developing adaptive self-management and coping skills and modifying their defenses

- breaking the connection between the behavior and specific triggers for the behavior

- building a support system.

Emily had previously dealt with issues related to her childhood sexual abuse, but had more recently followed a not unusual course of using excessive exercise as a "replacement" coping behavior for the food restricting (Something Fishy Website on Eating Disorders, 2005). Feelings of guilt, anxiety, low self-esteem, and loss of control of her life resulting from the sexual abuse and her eating disorder had provided a way for her to cope with these feelings. Continually challenging herself with doing more and more exercise alleviated guilt, reduced anxiety, and allowed her to feel in control of her life (at least immediately following a workout). Through counseling she realized that she was trying to build her still diminished self-image and self-respect, but that her life now was out of control in other ways. She and her therapist addressed the sexual abuse issues again. Emily identified and modified where necessary her beliefs and self-talk. She set behavioral goals related to decreasing her exercise and increasing time in other activities important to her. Emily had great self-discipline, which she had formerly applied to sports, eating restrictions, and exercise. She transformed this into working on her goals of spending more time with friends, being involved with outreach activities at church, and adding recreational time that included reading and going to movies.

Cross-Cultural Issues

Little is known about the prevalence of excessive exercise in the United States. Even statistics related to eating disorders are subject to question since physicians are not required to report them. Estimates based on research are that 1 percent of female adolescents have anorexia and 4 percent of college age females have bulimia. Ninety percent of those with eating disorders are female (*Anorexia Nervosa and Related Eating Disorders*, 2005). Adolescents between the ages of 11 and 17 are considered to be especially vulnerable, though adult onset is possible and cases of eating disorders have been reported in individuals even in their seventies. Eating disorders seem to be as likely in Hispanic-Americans as in European-American women; African-American women also experience eating disorders and seem to be more likely to develop bulimia than anorexia. As other countries become more Westernized and are exposed to media images of the "perfect body," which is thin for women and muscular for men (*Anorexia Nervosa and Related Eating Disorders*, 2005; Choi and Pitts, 2003), eating disorders seem to be on the increase (ANAD, 2005). However, statistics are few and are just estimates, and so one can only speculate as to the incidence of related excessive exercise behavior. However, severe food restricting has been shown to be associated with excessive exercising (Davis et al., 1999; Steffen and Brehm, 1999).

Results from a series of studies in South Africa suggest that the personality patterns of rigidity, inflexibility, and use of active rather than passive means of coping are associated with "excessive dependence on running"; a multidimensional approach is advised in future research because personality traits are not viewed as causal, but as interacting with other individual and contextual factors (Basson, 2001). A recent study of 257 college students in Pennsylvania found that nearly 22 percent were "exercise dependent," where this was rather broadly described as one who engaged in exercise at least 360 minutes per week and whose answers on a self-report questionnaire indicated an obligatory or pathological nature to their exercise activity (Garman et al., 2004). Further evidence that excessive exercise is becoming recognized as a public health issue is that the International Health, Racquet and Sportsclub Association, a trade organization in the fitness industry, has drafted guidelines to assist those in the industry (such as personal trainers, gym owners) in identifying and confronting individuals who appear to be exercising compulsively (Goodman, 2004).

In summary, little is known about the prevalence of excessive exercise in the United States, across cultures, or worldwide. According to the

Anorexia Nervosa and Related Eating Disorders website, "We have no idea how many people exercise compulsively" (*Anorexia Nervosa and Related Eating Disorders*, 2005); since this is the case, cross-cultural information is virtually non-existent.

Resources

Anorexia Nervosa and Related Eating Disorders; *www.anred.com*; an organization whose website provides information about eating disorders for both women and men, eating disorders of athletes, and treatment, recovery, relapse prevention, and statistics of eating disorders.

APA Help Center, an on-line service of the American Psychological Association for the general public, *helping.apa.org/articles/article.php?id=50*, provides articles and information about a variety of behavioral health issues including eating disorders.

National Association of Anorexia Nervosa and Associated Disorders (ANAD); P.O. Box 7, Highland Park, IL 60035; Hotline: (847) 831-3438; *www.anad.org*; a not-for-profit organization offering information about eating disorders, hotline counseling, a national network of support groups, treatment referrals, and education and prevention programs. It lobbies for state and national health insurance parity, supports research, and fights "dangerous advertising" that contributes to societal norms that promote eating disorders.

National Eating Disorders Association; 603 Stewart Street, Suite 803, Seattle, WA 98101; (206) 382-3587; Referral Helpline: (800) 931-2237; *www.NationalEatingDisorders.org*; is a not-for-profit organization working to prevent eating disorders. It provides general information about eating disorders, for both women and men, treatment referrals, information for parents and families of individuals with eating disorders, brochures, books, and a newsletter.

Something Fishy Website on Eating Disorders; *www.something-fishy.org*; provides information on eating disorders and related dangers, cultural issues, recovery. Offers information on compulsive exercising at *www.something-fishy.org/whatarethey/exercise.php*.

University of Pennsylvania, Office of Health Education; *www.vpul .upenn.edu/ohe/library/bodyimage/compulsive-exercise.htm*; an online service providing general medical and behavioral health information including questions and answers about compulsive exercising.

Helpful Books

The Anorexia Workbook: How to Accept Yourself, Heal Your Suffering, and Reclaim Your Life (Michelle Heffner and Georg H. Eifert, Oakland, CA: New Harbinger, 2004).

The BDD Workbook: Overcome Body Dysmorphic Disorder and End Body Image Obsession (James Claiborn and Cherry Pedrick, Oakland, CA: New Harbinger, 2002).

The Body Image Workbook: An 8-Step Program for Learning to Like Your Looks (Thomas F. Cash, Oakland, CA: New Harbinger, 1997).

Compulsive Exercise and the Eating Disorders: Toward an Integrated Theory of Activity (Alayne Yates, New York: Brunner/Mazel, 1991).

Eating Disorders: The Facts (Suzanne Abraham and Derek Llewellyn-Jones, New York: Oxford University Press, 1995).

Healing the Trauma of Abuse: A Woman's Workbook (Mary Ellen Copeland and Maxine Harris, Oakland, CA: New Harbinger, 2000).

The Overcoming Bulimia Workbook: Your Comprehensive Step-by-Step Guide to Recovery (Randi E. McCabe, Traci L. McFarlane, and Marion P. Olmsted, Oakland, CA: New Harbinger, 2003).

References

Abraham, S., and Llewellyn-Jones, D. (1995). *Eating disorders: The facts.* New York: Oxford University Press.

Adams, J. M., Miller, T. W., and Kraus, R. F. (2003). Exercise dependence: Diagnostic and therapeutic issues for patients in psychotherapy. *Journal of Contemporary Psychotherapy, 33,* 93–107.

American Psychiatric Association. (2000). *Diagnostic and statistical manual of mental disorders* (4th ed., text revision). Washington, DC: American Psychiatric Association.

Anorexia Nervosa and Related Eating Disorders. (2005). "Statistics: How many people have eating disorders?" Retrieved July 9, 2005, from *www.anred.com/stats.html.*

APA Help Center of the American Psychological Association. Retrieved July 9. 2005, from *helping.apa.org/articles/article.php?id=50.*

Basson, C. J. (2001). Personality and behaviour associated with excessive dependence on exercise: Some reflections from research. *South African Journal of Psychology, 31,* 53–60.

Choi, P. Y. L., and Pitts, M. (2003). In pursuit of male beauty: Physical exercise and the desire for muscularity. *Australian Journal of Psychology, 55,* 171. Abstract retrieved July 15, 2005, from EBSCO Host database.

Cox, R., and Orford, J. (2004). A qualitative study of the meaning of exercise for people who could be labeled as "addicted" to exercise — can "addiction" be applied to high frequency exercising? *Addiction Research and Theory, 12,* 167–188.

Davis, C. (1999). Excessive exercise and anorexia nervosa: Addictive and compulsive behaviors. *Psychiatric Annals, 29,* 221–224.

Davis, C. (2000). Exercise abuse. *International Journal of Sport Psychology, 31,* 278–289.

Davis, C., and Claridge, G. (1998). The eating disorders as addiction: A psychobiological perspective. *Addictive Behaviors, 23,* 463–475.

Davis, C., Kaptein, S., Kaplan, A. S., Olmsted, M. P., and Woodside, D. B. (1998). Obsessionality in anorexia nervosa: The moderating influence of exercise. *Psychosomatic Medicine, 60,* 192–197.

Davis, C., Katzman, D. K., and Kirsh, C. (1999). Compulsive physical activity in adolescents with anorexia nervosa. *Journal of Nervous and Mental Disease, 187,* 336–342.

Garman, J. F., Hayduk, D. M., Crider, D. A., and Hodel, M. M. (2004). Occurrence of exercise dependence in a college-aged population. *Journal of American College Health, 52,* 221–228.

Goodman, B. (2004, May/June). Stop that treadmill. *Psychology Today, 37,* 15.

Hausenblas, H. A., and Downs, D. S. (2002). How much is too much? The development and validation of the exercise dependence scale. *Psychology and Health, 17,* 387–404.

Hausenblas, H. A., and Fallon, E. A. (2002). Relationship among body image, exercise behavior, and exercise dependence symptoms. *International Journal of Eating Disorders, 32,* 179–185.

Lockwood, R., Lawson, R., and Waller, G. (2004). Compulsive features in the eating disorders: A role for trauma? *Journal of Nervous and Mental Disease, 192,* 247–249.

Loumidis, K., and Wells, A. (2001). Exercising for the wrong reasons: Relationships among eating disorder beliefs, dysfunctional exercise beliefs and coping. *Clinical Psychology and Psychotherapy, 8,* 416–423.

National Eating Disorder Association. (2005). *What causes eating disorders?* Retrieved July 9, 2005, from *www.NationalEatingDisorders.org.*

Nemours Foundation, KidsHealth website. *Compulsive exercise.* Retrieved on July 9, 2005, from *www.kidshealth.org/teen/exercise/problems/compulsive_exercise.htm.*

Office of Health Education, University of Pennsylvania. *Compulsive exercising.* Retrieved July 9, 2005, from *www.vpul.upenn.edu/ohe/library/bodyimage/compulsive-exercise.htm.*

Ogden, J., Veale, D., and Summers, Z. (1997). The development and validation of the exercise dependence questionnaire. *Addiction Research, 5,* 343–356.

Something Fishy Website on Eating Disorders. *Compulsive exercising.* Retrieved July 9, 2005, from *www.something-fishy.org/whatarethey/exercise.php.*

Steffen, J. J., and Brehm, B. J. (1999). The dimensions of obligatory exercise. *Eating Disorders, 7,* 1219–1226.

Steketee, G. (1999). *Overcoming obsessive-compulsive disorder.* Oakland, CA: New Harbinger.

Veale, D. M. W. DeCoverley. (1987). Exercise dependence. *British Journal of Addiction, 82,* 735–740.

Gambling

"There is a thrill, a feeling of ecstasy"

Dwight Presley and his family were the picture of middle-class success. In his late thirties and married with three children, he owned a home and had a good-paying position as an architect. It all began to unravel when strangers carted off the family SUV. Dwight had defaulted on a gambling loan, secured by the automobile that collectors came to recover.

His wife knew that he gambled for recreation during family vacations. That was no big deal to her, but what was hidden was that Dwight left his office nearly every afternoon to place bets at the racetrack. Some days he would forget to pick up the children from school, while he was squandering thousands of dollars at a time.

Dwight's wife found out about that at the same time she discovered that he had forged her name on loans and had taken out two mortgages. He had lost $60,000. Soon Dwight was without a family and a home. After 12 years of marriage, his wife packed up their children, aged ten, eight, and six, and left.

He went several months before gambling, but the lure of easy money soon became overpowering. He began to bet after work again. As his losses increased, Dwight found himself in an even deeper hole. Faced with a seemingly insurmountable wagering debt and nowhere to turn, Dwight embezzled from his employer. When the firm conducted an audit, Dwight was caught and ultimately sentenced to one year of house arrest and four years of probation. That was when Dwight knew he had to quit. He started going to Gamblers Anonymous (GA) and sought out Father Ladd, the priest at the church where GA meetings were held.

Pastoral Assessment It is imperative that the faith community understand gambling's negative effects on many individuals and their families. The conservative estimate is that there are 4 million persons with gambling problems in the United States (Ciarrocchi, 2001). While wagering continues to increase, its related problems are not well known in the United States, nor does the general public understand that gambling can be addictive. Americans spend more on gambling than on movies, sporting events, concerts, and theater combined (Vogel, 1997).

People need to be informed about the hidden costs of the "gaming" industry. Adult problem gamblers are more likely than the general population to divorce, have destabilized families, drink excessively and use drugs, abuse their spouses and children, suffer depression, and attempt suicide (Murray, 1993). The children of problem gamblers are more likely to do poorly in school; use illicit drugs, tobacco, and alcohol; run away; attempt suicide; indicate they are unhappy; and take up wagering than children from families where no one gambles (Ciarrocchi, 2001). Studies have found that the more parents bet, the greater the likelihood that the children will have problems with gambling (Wood and Griffiths, 1998). Three of four children of problem gamblers report that their first wagering experience occurred before the age of 11 (Freiberg, 1995).

Relevant History In 1988, only two states had large-scale casinos; now 27 states have them. Thirty-seven states operate a lottery, and some form of wagering is legal in 48 states. Advertisements for online gambling sites appear across the Internet. There are 280 websites that offer online wagering for real money (King, 1999). Internet bettors gambled at the rate of $2.3 billion in the United States in 1999, and this number is expected to grow to $10 billion worldwide in the near future (King, 1999; Singer, 2002). The rate of problems has continued to grow with increased access to legal wagering, especially in casinos, throughout the United States since the late 1980s. Researchers found a significant increase in rates of pathological gambling in studies conducted after 1994, compared with those done before 1994 (Shaffer et al., 1999).

Although the recent proliferation of wagering opportunities in the United States is intended for adults, research shows that adolescents are more likely to be problem gamblers than are adults. Wagering has been reported to be as high as 70 to 80 percent among adolescents, which makes it more popular among teens than alcohol use, cigarette smoking, or drug use (Kaminer et al., 2002; Shaffer and Hall, 1996). Studies have found links between adolescent problem gambling and several other issues, including substance abuse, juvenile delinquency, school difficulties, and psychological problems (National Research Council, 1999; Stinchfield and Winters, 1998).

Gambling fosters crime. In the three years following the opening of its first casino, Atlantic City's national ranking rose from fiftieth to first in per capita crime (Goodman, 1994). This rise in the crime rate following the introduction of legalized gambling in Atlantic City drove up the costs of courts and law enforcement at a rate five times faster than the average New Jersey county (Longman, 1994). Researchers are only beginning to understand the impact of wagering on youth growing up in societies where gambling is widely legal, accepted, marketed, and glamorized.

Diagnostic Criteria

Pathological gambling is a "persistent and recurrent maladaptive gambling behavior" that continues despite adverse consequences that are disruptive to one's life (American Psychiatric Association, 2000). In the United States the disorder is found in 1.4 to 1.9 percent of the adult population (Shaffer et al., 1999). Like substance abusers, pathological gamblers give up or jeopardize work, social, and family responsibilities in order to bet. The lifetime prevalence rate of pathological gambling exceeds that of cocaine and opioid use disorders (Regier et al., 1990).

Additionally, 2.9 to 4.8 percent of adults report problems because of their wagering but do not meet the full diagnostic criteria for pathological gambling. These individuals are identified as problem gamblers (Shaffer et al., 1999). Pathological and problem gamblers are more likely than recreational gamblers and nongamblers to have experienced a depressive episode, lost their job, been arrested, filed for bankruptcy, and been drug or alcohol dependent (National Research Council, 1999).

Men develop gambling disorders at about two to three times the rate of women, and ethnic minorities and persons of low socioeconomic status are overrepresented among pathological gamblers (National Research Council, 1999). Like the use of alcohol, gambling is a social activity for most people, but for a significant minority it is devastatingly addictive (American Psychiatric Association, 2000). Most compulsive gamblers say that they seek the "high" of betting through increasing the amounts of money they wager. They tend to "chase" the losses of one day with increased betting on the next day. Many pathological gamblers lie to family members, therapists, and others to hide their habit. Experts argue that gambling is the fastest growing addiction in the United States (Freiberg, 1995).

As wagering proliferates, it increases the exposure of youngsters to gambling and their vulnerability to the addiction. The market-savvy "gaming" industry is pushing the concept of "family entertainment centers," which include places for adults to wager while their children engage in other activities. The aim of the "gaming" industry is to create the next generation of gamblers from the children who watch their parents get excited by wagering. Researchers at Harvard Medical School reviewed nine studies of 7,700 young people, aged 15–20, in the United States and Canada (Shaffer and Hall, 1994). They found that 9.9 to 14.2 percent of the adolescents displayed problems with gambling and 4.4 to 7.4 percent met the diagnostic criteria for the disorder of "pathological gambling."

When Dwight spoke with Father Ladd he said, "I really never thought my gambling was a problem until I was facing prison time. I hit the bottom when the judge said that my crime could put me away for many years. It wasn't until then that it hit home." Dwight reported that his reasons for wagering were embedded in the excitement. "There is a thrill, a feeling of ecstasy," he explained. "I really didn't think it was a problem." Paradoxically, he thought that gambling "could fix some of my financial worries. You get to thinking that you can make that big win and pay off your debts and be worry-free."

Father Ladd was a good listener for Dwight and actively helped him to locate a mental health specialist to provide court-ordered specialized treatment. The priest knew his limitations, however, and he did not try to be the primary treatment professional for Dwight. Nevertheless, he said he would continue to support Dwight's efforts through Gamblers Anonymous (GA) and with the specialist.

With the assistance of Father Ladd, Dwight found an experienced therapist who used cognitive and behavioral therapies to aid him in reframing his thinking patterns. Dwight was also encouraged to change old habits that tended to promote gambling behavior. He was taught to identify and record situations that brought on the compulsion to wager and to recognize his distorted thinking that he could win against the odds. Two recent studies of Canadians who had a course of treatment for pathological gambling using a cognitive-behavioral model that included relapse prevention training reported a high success rate (Sylvain et al., 1997; Ladouceur et al., 2001).

Researchers have begun to find that religious involvement may be a protective factor against problem gambling. In a nationwide sample of U.S. adults, religious attendance was inversely associated with the risk of problem gambling (Hoffman, 2000). In a statewide survey, sociologists at the University of Texas found results suggesting that worship attendance and belief in the Bible are inversely associated with the frequency of playing the state lottery, as well as with the amount of money spent on the lottery (Ellison and Nybroten, 1999). In two other studies, among individuals in Nevada (Diaz, 2000) and Australia (Grichting, 1986), the frequency of wagering and the amount of money risked was discovered to be inversely related to the level of importance of religion for the person and the frequency of attendance at worship services.

If involvement in congregations lowers the risk of problem gambling, then encouraging youth and adults to be involved in religious life may be beneficial to those seeking to avoid wagering. Teens, for example, who participate in a religious youth group may find it a helpful place to experience peer support that can assist them in quitting gambling or in never starting. Faith-based intervention programs must address teens' abilities to recognize social and advertising pressures by the "gaming" industry, as well as helping them develop skills to resist such pressures.

Children must be taught that gambling is not a good way to gain independence or find fulfillment. The more youngsters are taught to believe in the importance of random chance and fate, the less they will believe in the values of diligence, industriousness, studiousness, and deferred gratification.

Indications for Referral Because wagering has largely been a hidden problem, few mental health professionals have had training in the assessment or treatment of pathological gambling and fewer still are aware of the wagering epidemic. Clergy may need to do considerable searching before they find a mental health specialist who has expertise in treating problem gambling. Pastors and other religious professionals who are informed about the plight of problem gamblers can help mental health professionals become more aware of the issue.

Treatment by Mental Health Specialist GA seems to be the most commonly used intervention among pathological gamblers. GA meetings increased 36 percent between 1995 and 1998, and there are now more than 1,000 chapters (National Research Council, 1999). Combining GA with professionally designed treatment may improve outcomes for pathological gamblers, as seems to be the case in the treatment of substance use disorders (Tonigan, Miller, and Connors, 2000).

Like drug abusers, compulsive gamblers tend to deny their problem and avoid finding help. GA is a 12-step program that encourages members to admit their problem and provides group support to help participants gain control over wagering. GA members recognize the denial and lies of the compulsive gambler and confront their distorted thinking. Family members may join Gam-Anon, which is modeled after Alanon, for group support. Compulsive gamblers must stop living in the fantasy world of their addiction and confront the reality of the consequences of their wagering.

Cross-Cultural Issues

Gambling is an international issue. In the U.K. the national lottery is played by more than two-thirds of British adults and illegally by about half of the adolescents (Reid et al., 1999; Pugh and Webley, 2000). For many teens in the U.K., wagering activities form a regular part of the weekly family entertainment (Wood and Griffiths, 1998). A recent study at the University of Exeter investigated illegal participation in the national lottery games by children under the age of 16 years in the county of Devon. The findings indicated that 56 percent of the sample had participated in the national lottery online game (Pugh and Webley, 2000). In a separate study of almost 1,200 youth (aged 11–15) conducted at Nottingham Trent University, it was found that 6 percent of the children fulfilled the criteria for the mental health disorder of pathological gambling, the majority of whom were males (Wood and Griffiths, 1998). These rates of addiction are twice as high as those reported among adults.

Resources

California Council on Problem Gambling; 800 South Harbor Boulevard, Suite 255, Anaheim, CA 92805; (800) GAMBLER or (800) 522-4700; *www.calproblemgambling.org*; a state-wide organization made up of individuals from clinical, academic, and research disciplines, as well as recovering compulsive gamblers and their families.

Chinese Community Problem Gambling Project; NICOS Chinese Health Coalition, 1208 Mason Street, San Francisco, CA 94108; (415) 788-6426; *www.nicoschc.com*; provides a problem gambling self-assessment in both Chinese and English, as well as articles in both languages.

Gamblers Anonymous (GA); P.O. Box 17173, Los Angeles, CA 90017; (213) 386-8789; *www.gamblersanonymous.org*; an international organization founded in 1957 with 1,200 chapters. It is a fellowship of men and women who share experiences, strength, and hope with each other to recover from compulsive gambling, following a 12-step program. GA publishes a monthly bulletin for members.

Institute for Research on Pathological Gambling and Related Disorders; Division on Addictions, Harvard Medical School, 10 President's Landing, 2nd Floor, Medford, MA 02215; (781) 306-8604; *www.divisiononaddictions.org/institute*; established in 2000 as a program of Harvard Medical School's Division on Addictions. Its mission is to alleviate the individual, social, medical, and economic burdens caused by pathological gambling through support of rigorous scientific research.

Know the Odds; P.O. Box 3079, Auburn, Victoria, Australia 3123; 0417-107-440; *www.knowodds.org*; provides educational materials to schools and colleges to help prevent the harmful effects of problem gambling.

National Center for Responsible Gambling; P.O. Box 14323, Washington, DC 20044-4323; (202) 530-4704; *www.ncrg.org*; founded in 1996 to help individuals and families affected by gambling disorders. It was the first national organization exclusively devoted to funding scientific research on pathological gambling.

National Coalition Against Legalized Gambling; 100 Maryland Avenue, NE, Room 311, Washington, DC 20002; (800) 664-2680;

www.ncalg.org; offers information on gambling and protests gambling expansion. The founder of the organization is a United Methodist minister, Thomas Grey.

National Council on Problem Gambling; 216 G Street, NE, Suite 200, Washington, DC 20002; (800) 522-4700; *www.ncpgambling.org*; is a non-profit health agency whose mission is to provide information about compulsive gambling and to promote the development of services for those suffering from pathological gambling.

North American Training Institute; 314 West Superior Street, Suite 702, Duluth, MN 55802; (888) 989-9234; *www.nati.org*; a division of the Minnesota Council on Compulsive Gambling. It has training programs for senior citizens and adolescents including *Wanna Bet* magazine for kids concerned about gambling.

Overcomers Outreach; P.O. 922950, Sylmar, CA 91392-2950; (800) 310-3001; *www.overcomersoutreach.org*; a Christian-oriented 12-step program with 1,000 support groups for teens with any type of compulsive behavior, including gambling.

Counseling Problem Gamblers and Their Families (Joseph W. Ciarrocchi, San Diego, CA: Academic Press, 2001).   **Helpful Books**

Don't Leave It to Chance: A Guide for Families of Problem Gamblers (Edward J. Federman, Charles E. Drebing, and Christopher Krebs, Oakland, CA: New Harbinger Publications, 2000).

Futures at Stake: Youth, Gambling, and Society (Howard J. Shaffer, Matthew N. Hall, Joni Vander Bilt, Elizabeth George, and Thomas N. Cummings, Las Vegas: University of Nevada Press, 2003).

The Gambling Addiction Patient Workbook (Robert R. Perkinson, New York: Sage Publications, 2003).

Understanding and Treating the Pathological Gambler (Robert Ladouceur, Caroline Sylvain, Claude Boutin, and Celine Doucet, New York: John Wiley and Sons, 2002).

References   American Psychiatric Association. (2000). *Diagnostic and statistical manual of mental disorders* (4th ed., text revision). Washington, DC: American Psychiatric Association.

Ciarrocchi, J. W. (2001). *Counseling problem gamblers and their families: A self-regulation manual for individual and family therapy.* San Diego, CA: Academic Press.

Diaz, J. D. (2000). Religion and gambling in Sin-City: A statistical analysis of the relationship between religion and gambling patterns in Las Vegas residents. *Social Science Journal,* 37(3), 453–458.

Ellison, C. G., and Nybroten, K. A. (1999). Conservative Protestants and opposition to state-sponsored lotteries: Evidence from the 1997 Texas poll. *Social Science Quarterly,* 80(2), 356–369.

Freiberg, P. (1995). Pathological gambling turning into epidemic. *American Psychological Association Monitor.* Retrieved on September 30, 1998, from *www.apa.org/monitor/dec95/gamblea.html.*

Goodman, R. (1994). *Legalized gambling as a strategy for economic development.* Amherst: University of Massachusetts–Amherst, Center for Economic Development.

Grichting, W. L. (1986). The impact of religion on gambling in Australia. *Australian Journal of Psychology,* 38(1), 45–58.

Hoffmann, J. P. (2000). Religion and problem gambling in the U.S. *Review of Religious Research,* 41(4), 488–509.

Kaminer, Y., Burleson, J. A., and Jadamec, A. (2002). Gambling behavior in adolescent substance abuse. *Substance Abuse,* 23(3), 191–198.

King, S. A. (1999). Internet gambling and pornography: Illustrative examples of the psychological consequences of communication anarchy. *CyberPsychology and Behavior,* 2(3), 175–193.

Ladouceur, R., Sylvain, C., Boutin, C., Lachance, S., Doucet, C., LeBlond, J., and Jacques, C. (2001). Cognitive treatment of pathological gambling. *Journal of Nervous and Mental Disease,* 189, 774–780.

Longman, P. (1994). The tax mirage. *Florida Trend,* June, 66–67.

Murray, J. B. (1993). Review of research on pathological gambling. *Psychological Reports,* 72, 791–810.

National Research Council. (1999). *Pathological gambling: A critical review.* Washington, DC: National Academy Press.

Pugh, P., and Webley, P. (2000). Adolescent participation in the U.K. national lottery games. *Journal of Adolescence,* 23(1), 1–11.

Regier, D. A., Farmer, M. E., Rae, D. S., Locke, B. Z., Keith, S. J., Judd, L. L., and Goodwin, F. K. (1990). Comorbidity of mental disorders with alcohol and other drug abuse: Results from the Epidemiologic Catchment Area (ECA) Study. *Journal of the American Medical Association,* 264, 2511–2518.

Reid, S., Woodford, S. J., Roberts, R., Golding, J. F., and Towell, A. D. (1999). Health-related correlates of gambling on the British National Lottery. *Psychological Reports,* Feb., 84(1), 247–254.

Shaffer, H. J., and Hall, M. N. (1996). Estimating the prevalence of adolescent gambling disorders: A quantitative synthesis and guide toward standard gambling nomenclature. *Journal of Gambling Studies,* 12(2), 193–214.

Shaffer, H. J., Hall, M. N., and Vander Bilt, J. (1999). Estimating the prevalence of disordered gambling behavior in the United States and Canada: A research synthesis. *American Journal of Public Health,* 89, 1369–1376.

Singer, H. W. (2002). High stakes on a little island. *Hosting Tech.* Retrieved September 8, 2003, from *www.hostingtech.com/browser/ 02_03_island.html.*

Stinchfield, R. D., and Winters, K. C. (1998). Adolescent gambling: A review of prevalence, risk factors and health implications. *Annals of the American Academy of Political and Social Science,* 556, 172–185.

Sylvain, C., Ladouceur, R., and Boisvert, J. (1997). Cognitive and behavioral treatment of pathological gambling: A controlled study. *Journal of Consulting and Clinical Psychology,* 65(5), 727–732.

Tonigan, J. S., Miller, W. R., and Connors, G. J. (2000). Project MATCH client impressions about Alcoholics Anonymous: Measurement issues and relationship to treatment outcome. *Alcoholism Treatment Quarterly,* 18, 25–41.

Vogel, J. (1997). *Crapped out: How gambling ruins the economy and destroys lives.* Monroe, ME: Common Courage Press.

Wood, R. T., and Griffiths, M. D. (1998). The acquisition, development and maintenance of lottery and scratchcard gambling in adolescence. *Journal of Adolescence,* 21(3), 265–273.

Heroin

"She turned into an out-of-control alien"

Kathy had been a child full of adventure who had spent her early years in ballet, Girl Scouts, and the church children's choir. Unfortunately, Kathy did not develop a strong sense of self-confidence and tended to look to her classmates for direction and approval. Under peer pressure she first tried cigarettes and alcohol and then marijuana at 15 and heroin at 16. She was not aware that it was heroin when some boys gave it to her to try. From that point on, her life and her family's radically changed.

Kathy turned into a completely different person. There was constant turmoil in the household. Her behavior became a continuous pattern of lying and stealing to obtain money to buy the drug. She turned into an alien, an alien who was out of control. Her addiction placed her parents and their marriage under intense stress. The power of the drug was cracking the family apart and killing the child. Kathy is now threatening to take her life with an overdose. Her parents sought out their pastor for guidance.

Clergy are more likely to see families who have a child using heroin today than was the case even ten years ago. The incidence of the use of heroin and other opioids like OxyContin (see p. 117) among teens has doubled since the early 1990s. Heroin abuse in the United States has reached levels not seen since the 1960s (U.S. Department of Health and Human Services, 2002). Opioids are the second most commonly

Pastoral Assessment

abused group of illicit substances; only marijuana use is more prevalent. According to the national school-based study *Monitoring the Future*, 1.6 percent of 8th graders, 1.8 percent of 10th graders, and 1.7 percent of 12th graders surveyed reported using heroin at least once during their lifetime (U.S. Department of Health and Human Services, 2002). This noticeable increase in the number of youth using heroin is probably the result of its reduced cost.

Relevant History   Opioids are the most powerful known pain relievers. Their use and abuse date back to antiquity (Gahlinger, 2001). Their pain-relieving and euphoric effects were known to the Sumerians (4000 B.C.) and the Egyptians (2000 B.C.). The substance was also used by the ancient Greeks, who named it *opion* ("poppy juice"), from which the present name is derived.

Heroin was first synthesized in 1874 by a British chemist working in London (Gahlinger, 2001). It comes from morphine, a naturally occurring substance extracted from the seed pod of certain types of poppy plants (Kaplan and Sadock, 1998). Bayer Laboratories in Germany registered *Heroin* (meaning "heroic treatment" from the German word *heroisch*) as a trademark. From 1898 through 1910 it was marketed as a non-addictive morphine substitute and cough medicine for children. In 1914 the Harrison Narcotic Act made it illegal to manufacture or possess heroin in the United States. Heroin traffic is worldwide, and the biggest producer is Afghanistan (Gahlinger, 2001). It continues to be illegal for any purpose in the United States, while it is legally used by cancer patients in the United Kingdom and some other countries (Kaplan and Sadock, 1998).

Diagnostic Criteria   Heroin is illegally used as a powerful and addictive drug producing intense euphoria (American Psychiatric Association, 2000). Its popularity with recreational users probably comes from its especially rapid onset. Heroin can be smoked ("chasing the dragon"), snorted, or injected. It is quickly metabolized by the brain, becoming morphine

OXYCONTIN

In some areas of the country OxyContin abuse is a greater problem than heroin abuse (Cicero et al., 2005). OxyContin is a semisynthetic opioid prescribed for long-lasting pain (Gahlinger, 2001). The medication's active ingredient is called oxycodone. OxyContin is called "Oxy," "O.C.," and "killer" on the street. It is prescribed as a timed-release tablet and can provide as many as 12 hours of relief from chronic pain. It is often prescribed for cancer and arthritis patients, or those suffering from long-term back pain (Kalso, 2005). The benefit of the medication to chronic pain patients is that they generally need to take the pill only twice a day. OxyContin abusers either crush the tablet and ingest or snort it or dilute it in water and inject it. Crushing or diluting the tablet removes the timed-release action of the medication and causes a quick, powerful high. Abusers have compared this feeling to the euphoria they experience when taking heroin. Addiction to OxyContin is so strong that people will go to great lengths to get the drug, including robbing pharmacies and forging prescriptions. Other drugs in the opiate family that are abused include codeine, hydrocodone, morphine, thebaine, tilidine, anileridine, etorphine, and fentanyl (Gahlinger, 2001).

(Kaplan and Sadock, 1998). The morphine molecule then binds with brain receptors, which produces the "high." Users tend to report feeling a "rush" or a surge of pleasurable sensations (Gahlinger, 2001).

The feeling varies in intensity depending on how much of the drug is ingested and how rapidly the drug enters the brain and binds to the natural opioid receptors (Gahlinger, 2001). The "rush" is usually accompanied by a warm flushing of the skin, a dry mouth, and a heavy feeling in the user's arms and legs. A person may also experience nausea, vomiting, and severe itching. Following the initial effects, an individual will be drowsy for several hours with poor mental function and a slow heart rate (Gahlinger, 2001).

Pure heroin is a white powder with a bitter taste. Most comes in powdered form in colors ranging from white to dark brown. The colors are caused by impurities left from the manufacturing process or the presence of additives. "Black tar" is a form of heroin that resembles roofing tar or is hard like coal. Its color varies from dark brown to black (Gahlinger, 2001).

Repeated heroin use produces physical dependence, which causes a user's body to adapt to the presence of the drug and withdrawal symptoms to occur if use is reduced (American Psychiatric Association, 2000). Physical dependence is expected after two to ten days of continuous use when the drug is stopped suddenly. Heroin withdrawal symptoms usually peak within 36–72 hours and may last for 7–14 days (APA, 2000).

Symptoms of withdrawal begin within a few hours and can include restlessness, muscle and bone pain, insomnia, diarrhea, vomiting, cold flashes, and involuntary leg movements (APA, 2000). The death rate for those who use heroin and other opiates is higher than that of people who use other powerful illicit drugs, such as cocaine and phencyclidine (PCP).

Response to Vignette

Kathy is in a crisis situation that will likely require immediate inpatient care. When substance abuse is associated with danger to self (such as talk of suicide by overdose) or other anti-social behavior (such as lying and stealing), inpatient care is usually the required treatment modality (APA, 2000). Voluntary admission to inpatient care has the best chance for a positive outcome. Although it may be necessary in some cases, involuntary hospitalization is a last resort, since it reduces the chance of future treatment compliance.

The family's pastor had educated herself about mental health resources in the area and was prepared to help the couple find a psychiatrist who specialized in adolescent substance abuse issues. The specialist quickly assessed the crisis situation and Kathy agreed to inpatient treatment.

Adolescence is a period of dramatic psychological change and adjustment, marked by increased autonomy from parents and more reliance on peers for direction and validation (Weaver et al., 2001). As a result of peer pressure many teens experiment with substances, including tobacco and alcohol. Unfortunately, in some cases the recreational use of "gateway substances" can be followed by the use of dangerous illicit drugs such as opiates (Kaplan and Sadock, 1998). Adolescents who have emotionally supportive parents with open communication styles and who actively monitor their children's activities with awareness of their children's potential for use of substances may have some protection from drug abuse. Involvement in organized school activities and academic achievement are also related to lower risk for substance abuse (Patton, 1995).

Treatment within the Faith Community

Faith communities need to recognize the potential value of religion in the lives of individuals suffering from a variety of difficult problems, including persons in recovery from addiction. Researchers in California examined the relation between religious faith, spirituality, and mental health in 236 individuals recovering from substance abuse. They found that higher levels of religious faith and spirituality were associated with several positive factors, including a more optimistic life perspective, greater social support, higher resilience to stress, and lower levels of anxiety (Pardini et al., 2000).

In a study using a nationwide sample of patients being treated for opiate addiction in 18 clinics from 11 urban areas, researchers found that almost half (47 percent) of the 432 patients said religion/spirituality was a significant factor in their recovery (Flynn et al., 2003). Those who were in recovery for at least five years indicated that religion/spirituality was almost as important in accounting for their positive changes as the medical treatment. Other significant factors for the recovering patients over the five years were personal motivation, family, and their job or career (Flynn et al., 2003).

People of faith need to understand that religious involvement can be an important preventive factor for youth who are tempted to abuse substances. A national study of teens in grades 7–12 measured frequency of attendance at religious services, participation in religious youth group activities, frequency of prayer, and importance of religion (Nonnemaker et al., 2003). The researchers found that both public and private religious activities were protective factors against cigarette, alcohol, and marijuana use.

Indications for Referral

This crisis situation involving a dangerous and illicit drug is a good example of how a pastor who is informed about mental health specialists in the community can help those in need of immediate assistance. A knowledgeable clergyperson understands that a timely referral is an act of responsible and valuable pastoral care. Clergy often serve most effectively in the mental health network as skilled facilitators, identifying the needs of persons and connecting them to a larger circle of specialized helpers.

Treatment by Mental Health Specialist

Withdrawal therapy or detoxification is used to relieve the symptoms experienced when heroin use is discontinued, and it is used to aid the transition to long-term treatment (Kaplan and Sadock, 1998). The goal of detoxification is to help a person stop taking the addicting drug as quickly and safely as possible. This may involve gradually reducing the dose of the drug or temporarily substituting other substances, such as methadone, that have less severe side effects (Kaplan and Sadock, 1998). For some individuals, it may be safe to undergo withdrawal therapy on an outpatient basis; others will require placement in a hospital or a residential treatment center.

There is a range of treatment options for heroin addicts like Kathy, including medications and behavioral therapies. Methadone has been used to treat heroin addiction for more than three decades (Amato et al., 2005). This synthetic narcotic suppresses withdrawal symptoms for 24 to 36 hours. Although a person remains physically dependent on the opioid, the craving for heroin is reduced and the highs and lows are blocked. This permits a patient to be free from the disruptive behavior associated with addiction (Amato et al., 2005).

Other pharmaceutical approaches to heroin treatment include naloxone and naltrexone, LAAM (levo-alpha-acetyl-methadol), and buprenorphine (Vocci et al., 2005). Buprenorphine is a particularly promising treatment because, compared with other medications such as methadone, it causes weaker opiate effects and is less likely to have overdose complications.

Several behavioral treatments, such as contingency management therapy and cognitive-behavioral interventions are useful. Contingency management therapy uses a voucher system, where individuals earn "points" based on negative drug tests, which they can exchange for items that encourage healthy living (Silverman, 1996). Cognitive-behavioral interventions are designed to help modify the patient's expectations and behaviors related to drug use and to increase skills in coping with various life stressors.

Cross-Cultural Issues

According to a national survey, heroin addiction accounted for 15.2 percent of all treatment admissions to hospitals in 2000 (243,523 admissions). Males were in the majority, accounting for more than two of three of the admissions at 66.9 percent (SAMHSA, 2002). Treatment admissions by race/ethnicity ranged from 47.3 percent for European-Americans to 24.7 percent for Hispanic-Americans to 24.2 percent for African-Americans. Almost 80 percent of heroin admissions had been in treatment before the current episode and 25 percent had been in treatment five or more times (SAMHSA, 2002).

Resources

American Academy of Child and Adolescent Psychiatry has a website with free information on teen problems, including drug abuse, at *www.aacap.org*.

American Council for Drug Education; 164 West 74th Street, New York, NY 10023; (800) 883-DRUG; *www.acde.org*.

American Psychiatric Association; 1400 K Street, NW, Washington, DC 20005; (202) 682-6000; *www.psych.org.*

American Psychological Association; 750 First Street, NE, Washington, DC 20002; (202) 336-5500; *www.apa.org.*

Hazelden Foundation; Box 176, Center City, MN 55012; (800) 257-7810; *www.hazelden.org.*

Narcotics Anonymous; P.O. Box 9999, Van Nuys, CA 91409; (818) 773-9999; *www.na.org.*

National Institute on Drug Abuse; National Institutes of Health, 6001 Executive Boulevard, Room 5213, Bethesda, MD 20892-9561; (301) 443-1124; *www.drugabuse.gov.*

Helpful Books

Buprenorphine Therapy of Opiate Addiction (Pascal Kintz, Albert D. Fraser, and Pierre Marquet, Totowa, NJ: Humana Press, 2002).

Dark Paradise: A History of Opiate Addiction in America (David T. Courtwright, Cambridge, MA: Harvard University Press, 2001).

Methadone Matters: Evolving Practice of Community Methadone Treatment of Opiate Addiction (Gillian Tober and John Strang, New York: Taylor and Francis, 2003).

New Treatments for Opiate Dependence (Susan M. Stine and Thomas R. Kosten, New York: Guilford Publications, 1997).

Opiates (Nancy Harris, Farmington Hills, MI: Thomson Gale, 2005).

References

Amato, L., Davoli, M., Perucci, C. A., Ferri, M., Faggiano, F., and Mattick, R. P. (2005). An overview of systematic reviews of the effectiveness of opiate maintenance therapies: Available evidence to inform clinical practice and research. *Journal of Substance Abuse Treatment,* 28(4), 321–329.

American Psychiatric Association. (2000). *Diagnostic and statistical manual of mental disorders* (4th edition, text revision). Washington, DC: American Psychiatric Association.

Cicero, T. J., Inciardi, J. A., and Munoz, A. (2005). Trends in abuse of Oxycontin and other opioid analgesics in the United States: 2002–2004. *Journal of Pain,* 6(10), 662–672.

Flynn, P. M., Joe, G. W., Broome, K. M., Simpson, D. D., and Brown, B. S. (2003). Recovery from opioid addiction in DATOS. *Journal of Substance Abuse Treatment,* 25(3), 177–186.

Gahlinger, P. M. (2001). *Illegal drugs: A complete guide to their history, chemistry, use and abuse.* Ogden, UT: Sagebrush Press.

Kalso, E. (2005). Oxycodone. *Journal of Pain Symptom Management,* 29(5 Suppl.), S47–56.

Kaplan, H. I., and Sadock, B. J. (1998). *Synopsis of psychiatry: Behavioral sciences/clinical psychiatry,* 8th edition. Baltimore: Williams and Wilkins.

Nonnemaker, J. M., McNeely, C. A., and Blum, R. W. (2003). Public and private domains of religiosity and adolescent health risk behaviors: Evidence from the National Longitudinal Study of Adolescent Health. *Social Science and Medicine,* 57(11), 2049–2054.

Pardini, D., Plante, T., Sherman, A., and Stump, J. (2000). Religious faith and spirituality in substance abuse recovery: Determining the mental health benefits. *Journal of Substance Abuse Treatment,* 19, 347–354.

Patton, L. H. (1995). Adolescent substance abuse: Risk factors and protective factors. *Pediatric Clinics of North America,* 42(2), 283–293.

Silverman, K., Wong, C. J., Higgins, S. T., Brooner, R. K., Montoya, I. D., Contoreggi, C., et al. (1996). Increasing opiate abstinence through voucher-based reinforcement therapy. *Drug and Alcohol Dependence,* 41, 157–165.

Substance Abuse and Mental Health Services Administration (SAMHSA) (2002). *Treatment episode data set 1992–2000: National admissions to substance abuse treatment services.* Retrieved online at *www.oas.samhsa.gov/dasis.htm#teds2.*

U.S. Department of Health and Human Services. (2002). *Monitoring the Future Study*. Rockville, MD: National Institute on Drug Abuse.

Vocci, F. J., Acri, J., and Elkashef, A. (2005). Medication development for addictive disorders: The state of the science. *American Journal of Psychiatry,* 162(8) 1432–1440.

Weaver, A. J., Revilla, L. A., and Koenig, H. G. (2001). *Counseling families across the stages of life: A handbook for pastors and other helping professionals*. Nashville: Abingdon Press.

Inhalants

"His sudden, senseless death was shocking"

Rev. Briscoe found this a particularly difficult and personally painful funeral to conduct at his small Lutheran church. The 14-year-old boy was the only child of the active and beloved Kraus family. He was an exceptionally gifted, athletic teenager with immense personal charm and promise. Simeon Kraus was found unconscious in a neighbor's backyard. According to his three companions, the four teenagers had, on a dare, taken gas from a barbeque grill's propane tank. The boys put the gas in a plastic bag and inhaled it to get high. Simeon collapsed shortly after breathing from the bag. Cardiopulmonary resuscitation failed to revive him, and he was declared dead at the hospital.

The Kraus family and the congregation were devastated by the senseless and sudden tragedy. The death was incomprehensible and constantly impinged upon the thoughts of his parents, Kathy and Steve. At the funeral they told Rev. Briscoe that they felt as though "they were just going through the motions of their daily lives and none of it made much sense."

Shortly after the death, Rev. Briscoe visited a close pastoral colleague, Rev. Swecker, a Disciples of Christ pastor, in a neighboring town to talk about the ordeal. His friend told him that he had had a similar experience less than two years ago. He had done a memorial service for an 11-year-old girl who lived in his community. The child had been inhaling fumes from cleaning fluid while at school and became ill a few minutes afterward. Witnesses alerted the parents, and the girl was hospitalized and placed on life support systems. She died 48 hours after the incident.

Pastoral Assessment   Inhalant abuse is like playing Russian roulette. There is the real danger of devastating medical consequences, including death (Anderson and Loomis, 2003). Sniffing of the highly concentrated chemicals in solvents or aerosol sprays can induce irregular and rapid heart rhythms and lead to heart failure and death within minutes of a session of sniffing (Anderson and Loomis, 2003). This syndrome, known as "sudden sniffing death," which killed Simeon, can result from a single session of inhalant use by an otherwise healthy young person. Sudden sniffing death is particularly associated with the abuse of propane, butane, and chemicals in aerosols. Inhalant abuse also can cause death by asphyxiation — from repeated inhalations, which lead to high concentrations of inhaled fumes replacing oxygen in the lungs; suffocation — from blocking air from entering the lungs when inhaling fumes from a plastic bag placed over the head; choking — from inhalation of vomit after inhalant use; or fatal injury — from accidents.

Young people are particularly likely to abuse inhalants because they are easily available, inexpensive, hard to detect, and work immediately. Furthermore, their abuse carries no criminal penalties. Children and adolescents can walk into almost any grocery store, hardware store, or pharmacy and pick them off the shelf. These factors make inhalants, for some youth, one of the first substances to be abused (Kurtzman et al., 2001).

Children and adolescents are often unaware of the health threats posed by inhalation of solvents, and the less knowledgeable they are of the risks the more likely they are to use them (Johnston et al., 1998). Inhalant abusers include both sexes and all socioeconomic groups throughout the United States. Surveys consistently show that nearly one in five children in middle school and high school has experimented with inhaled substances (U.S. Department of Health and Human Services, 2003). It is not unusual to see elementary and middle school–aged youths involved with inhalant abuse. In fact most inhalant users are between 11 and 14 years of age (Burk, 2001). Education of children and parents is essential to decrease experimentation with inhalants.

Relevant History

According to a nationwide annual survey of drug use among 8th, 10th, and 12th graders, inhalant use by 8th graders increased significantly in 2003, following a previous decline in use in all three grades (U.S. Department of Health and Human Services, 2003). Between 1995 and 2002, 8th graders' annual rate of use fell from 12.8 percent to 7.7 percent, as an increasing proportion of students became aware that inhalant use is dangerous. However, 8th graders' use rose to 8.7 percent in 2003. In addition there was an alarming increase in emergency department admissions of inhalant use victims, up 187 percent, from 522 in 2001 to 1,496 in 2002 (Drug Abuse Warning Network, 2003).

Diagnostic Criteria

Inhalants are breathable chemical vapors that produce psychoactive (mind-altering) effects. The term "inhalant" covers a broad range of chemicals found in hundreds of different products that may have different pharmacological effects (Anderson and Loomis, 2003). Inhalants can be breathed in through the nose or the mouth in several ways, including "sniffing" or "snorting" fumes from containers, spraying aerosols directly into the nose or mouth, inhaling fumes from substances sprayed or deposited inside a plastic or paper bag, "huffing" from an inhalant soaked rag stuffed in the mouth, and inhaling from balloons filled with nitrous oxide.

These methods of delivery mean that the chemicals are rapidly absorbed through the lungs into the bloodstream and quickly distributed to the brain and other organs. Within minutes of inhalation, a user experiences intoxication along with other effects similar to those produced by alcohol, including slurred speech, lightheadedness, an inability to coordinate movements, euphoria, and dizziness. After heavy use, abusers may feel drowsy for several hours and experience a lingering headache (Anderson and Loomis, 2003).

Inhalant use can become addictive, and chronic abuse can damage the heart, lungs, liver, kidneys, and nervous system. Inhalant use during pregnancy can cause fetal abnormalities. Diagnosis of inhalant abuse is difficult and relies almost entirely on a detailed history. No specific laboratory tests confirm solvent inhalation. Treatment is generally supportive counseling, because there are no reversal agents for inhalant intoxication (Anderson and Loomis, 2003).

Children and adolescents can readily find products to use as inhalants. Many people do not think of these items as drugs because they were never meant to be used to achieve an intoxicating effect. Yet, children and teens can easily obtain these exceedingly toxic substances. These inhalants fall into several groupings:

1. **Solvents** are found in a multitude of inexpensive, easily available products used for common household and industrial purposes such as:

   - **Adhesives**: model airplane glue, rubber cement, household glue

   - **Aerosols**: spray paint, hairspray, air freshener, deodorant, fabric protector

   - **Solvents and gases**: nail polish remover, paint thinner, typing correction fluid and thinner, toxic markers, pure toluene, gasoline, carburetor cleaner, octane booster, cigarette lighter fluid

   - **Cleaning agents**: dry cleaning fluid, spot remover, degreaser

   - **Food products**: vegetable cooking spray, dessert topping spray (whipped cream), whippets

2. **Gases** include medical anesthetics, as well as gases used in household or commercial products — butane, propane, helium. Medical anesthetic gases include ether, chloroform, halothane, and nitrous oxide, commonly called "laughing gas."

3. **Nitrites**: Aliphatic nitrites, including cyclohexyl nitrite, an ingredient found in room deodorizers; amyl nitrite "poppers" or "snappers" used for medical purposes; and butyl nitrite "rush," "locker room," "bolt," or "climax," also marketed in head shops as "video head cleaner." Unlike most other inhalants, which act directly on the central nervous system, nitrites act primarily to dilate blood vessels and relax the muscles. While other inhalants are used to alter mood, nitrites are used primarily as sexual enhancers.

The death of a child is among the most emotionally painful of experiences. Parents, other family members, and friends go through a predictable period of grieving in the aftermath of an unexpected loss. Uncomplicated bereavement is an essential emotional response to human loss. Although incredibly painful, it is not considered pathological, and it actually appears to be essential for eventual psychological healing to occur (Weaver and Stone, 2005). All religious caregivers are familiar with the typical responses seen during bereavement (for example, sadness, loneliness). **Response to Vignette**

It is important to note that following a loss, a significant minority of people, especially family members, will experience some type of *complicated bereavement*. The most common forms of this include: inhibited bereavement (persistent numbing and lack of an emotional response, often accompanied by physical symptoms such as tension, insomnia, and/or increased substance use/abuse), serious depression, and *traumatic bereavement*. For example, acute stress and post-traumatic stress disorder (PTSD) are common in relatives of suicide victims (36 percent develop such symptoms) and are found in 14 percent of the loved ones of those who die very unexpectedly (Zisook et al., 1999).

There is considerable evidence showing that faith is widely used and can help ease the effect of the death of a loved one (Weaver and Stone,

2005). Studies in California (Davis et al., 1998) and Great Britain (Walsh et al., 2002) have shown a positive relationship between religious involvement and adapting to the loss of a family member or close friend. Researchers found that individuals grieving the death of a family member or close friend reported a strong linkage between positive psychological adjustment and one's ability to make sense of the loss through one's faith.

Treatment within the Faith Community

After the tragic death of two children in their communities, Rev. Briscoe and Rev. Swecker decided that they would educate themselves and their churches on the dangers of inhalant abuse. They discovered that one of the most important steps that parents can take is to encourage their children not to experiment even a first time with inhalants. Children must be told about the serious risks in abusing these dangerous substances. It is important to emphasize that inhalants are deadly chemicals and poisons. In addition, it is helpful to communicate with teachers, guidance counselors, and coaches for them to become more aware of the dangers. By discussing the problem of inhalants openly and stressing the devastating consequences of their abuse, one can help prevent a tragedy. Because awareness of the problem was low in their area, the churches in this case launched an inhalant prevention campaign involving the local newspapers, law enforcement, schools, and civic organizations.

Indications for Referral

A referral to a mental health specialist should be made for parents, other family members, or friends who have not been able to return to normal routines several weeks after the death of a young person. People who need a referral may remain withdrawn from personal relationships, be preoccupied with thoughts about the death, and continue to feel helpless and hopeless. Pastors need the skills to recognize when a person is in distress from overwhelming grief and requires a mental health specialist.

Treatment for inhalant abuse must be well targeted. Standard alcohol and drug treatments are not usually effective for inhalant abusers. Mental health professionals also need to understand the unique aspects of the problem, including a slow rate of recovery and the minimal improvements that should initially be expected. Even experienced mental health professionals may not be fully aware of the toxicity and lethality of inhalants.

Treatment by Mental Health Specialist

Family involvement in treatment is crucial. This includes education about inhalants, removal of inhalants from the home, and understanding of the continuing support and supervision that inhalant abusers will need. It is helpful to have a school counselor involved in the treatment plan to assist the family and user.

Inhalant abuse is an international problem, particularly among young people who are poor. For example, Native youth living in North American, reservations or other rural areas in substandard conditions report unusually high rates of inhalant use. Researchers in Canada found that Native youth in grades 7–12 were more likely to abuse inhalants than European-American cohorts (Gfellner and Hundleby, 1995). In a second study Australian Aborigines and reservation-based Canadian and American Indians were found to be particularly inclined to inhalant abuse because of the low cost and easy availability (Dinwiddle, 1994). In the United States users are more likely to be European-American, Hispanic-American, or Native-American than African-American or Asian-American (Burk, 2001).

Cross-Cultural Issues

American Academy of Addiction Psychiatry; 1010 Vermont Avenue, NW, Suite 710, Washington, DC 20005; (202) 393-4484; *www.aaap .org*.

Resources

American Academy of Child and Adolescent Psychiatry; 3615 Wisconsin Avenue, NW, Washington, DC 20016; (202) 966-7300; *www.aacap.org*; has a website with free information on teen problems, including drugs.

American Council for Drug Education; 164 West 74th Street, New York, NY 10023; (800) 883-DRUG; *www.acde.org*.

American Society of Addiction Medicine; 4601 North Park Avenue, Upper Arcade #101, Chevy Chase, MD 20815; (301) 656-3920; *www.asam.org*; is a medical society dedicated to educating physicians and improving the treatment of individuals suffering from alcoholism and other addictions.

Hazelden Foundation; Box 176, Center City, MN 55012; (800) 257-7810; *www.hazelden.org*.

National Center on Addiction and Substance Abuse at Columbia University; 633 Third Avenue, 19th floor, New York, NY 10017; (212) 841-5200; *www.casacolumbia.org*.

National Clearinghouse for Alcohol and Drug Information; P.O. Box 2345, Rockville, MD 20847; (800) 729-6686; *www.health*.org; provides free, useful materials about the many aspects of adolescent alcohol and drug abuse treatment and prevention. Several of these publications are designed for the faith community.

National Inhalant Prevention Coalition; 322–A Thompson Street, Chattanooga, TN 37405; (800) 269-4237; *www.inhalants.org*.

National Institute on Drug Abuse, National Institutes of Health; 6001 Executive Boulevard, Room 5213, Bethesda, MD 20892-9561; (301) 443-1124; *www.drugabuse.gov*.

Partnership for a Drug-Free America; 405 Lexington Avenue, Suite 1601, New York, NY 10174; (212) 922-1560; *www.drugfree.org*.

Rainbows; 2100 Golf Road #370, Rolling Meadows, IL 60008; (800) 266-3206; *www.rainbows.org*; an international organization with 6,300 affiliated groups. Founded in 1983, Rainbows establishes peer support groups in churches, schools, and social agencies for children and adults who are grieving a divorce, death, or other painful change in their family. The groups are led by trained adults, and referrals are provided.

Concepts of Chemical Dependency (Harold E. Doweiko, London: **Helpful** Wadsworth Press. 2001). **Books**

Danger: Inhalants [ages 5–9] (Ruth Chier, New York: Rosen Publishing Group, 2003).

Grief Counseling and Grief Therapy: A Handbook for the Mental Health Professional (J. William Worden, New York: Springer Publishing, 2001).

Inhalants and Solvents [ages 12 and up] (Linda Bayer-Berenbaum and Steven L. Jaffe, New York: Chelsea House, 1999).

Reflections on Grief and Spiritual Growth (Andrew J. Weaver and Howard W. Stone, Nashville: Abingdon Press, 2005).

Anderson, C. A., and Loomis, G. A. (2003). Recognition and preven- **References** tion of inhalant abuse. *American Family Physician, 68*, 869–876.

Burk, I. (2001). *Inhalant Prevention Resource Guide.* Richmond: Virginia Department of Education.

Davis, C. G., Nolen-Hocksema, S., and Larson, J. (1998). Making sense of loss and benefiting from the experience: Two construals of meaning. *Journal of Personality and Social Psychology, 75*(2), 561–574.

Dinwiddle, S. H. (1994). Abuse of inhalants: A review. *Addiction, 89*, 925–939.

Drug Abuse Warning Network (DAWN). (2003). Mortality Data 2002. Rockville, MD: U.S. Department of Health and Human Services, Substance Abuse and Mental Health Services Administration, *www.dawninfo.samhsa.gov/pubs_94_02/mepubs/default.asp.*

Gfellner, B. M., and Hundleby, J. D. (1995). Patterns of drug use among Native and White adolescents: 1990–1993. *Canadian Journal of Public Health, 86*, 95–97.

Johnston, L., O'Malley, P., and Bachman, J. (1998). *National survey results on drug use from the Monitoring the Future Study, 1975–1997.* Rockville, MD: National Institute on Drug Abuse.

Kurtzman, T. L., Otsuka, K. N., and Wahl, R. A. (2001). Inhalant abuse by adolescents. *Journal of Adolescent Health,* 28(3), 170–180.

U.S. Department of Health and Human Services. (2003). *Monitoring the Future Study.* Rockville, MD: National Institute on Drug Abuse.

Walsh, K., King, M., Jones, L., Tookman, A., and Blizard, R. (2002). Spiritual beliefs may affect outcome of bereavement: Prospective study. *British Medical Journal,* 324, 1551–1554.

Weaver, A. J., and Stone, H. W. (2005). *Reflections on grief and spiritual growth.* Nashville: Abingdon Press.

Zisook, S., Chentsova-Dutton, Y., and Shuchter, S. R. (1999). PTSD following bereavement. *Annals of Clinical Psychiatry,* 10(4), 157–163.

Marijuana

"The teenagers saw marijuana as a harmless substance"

Rev. Mike Kidd was the youth pastor in a large urban church. Recently he had given an anonymous survey to his junior high and high school youth groups. He was surprised by the large number of adolescents who had either tried marijuana or knew someone who had smoked it. Even more surprising to Rev. Kidd were the attitudes among the youth regarding the use of cannabis. Many saw marijuana as a harmless substance that could be used without negative consequences. The youth pastor decided to research the topic himself so he could be better informed. After educating himself about cannabis, he decided to offer a class to the youth groups about what he discovered.

Pastoral Assessment

Rev. Kidd's research taught him that marijuana is the most commonly used illicit drug in the United States. According to the 2004 National Survey on Drug Use and Health more than four in ten Americans over the age of 12 have tried it sometime in their lives (SAMHSA, 2005). The same study found that 25.5 million people used marijuana in the previous year and 14.6 million people used it in the past month. Additionally, the research found that a large group, 3.2 million Americans, used it on a daily or almost daily basis over the previous year (SAMHSA, 2005).

Marijuana is a green or brown mixture of dried, shredded leaves, stems, seeds, and flowers of the hemp plant. "Cannabis" is a term that refers to marijuana and other drugs made from the same plant, including hashish (hash), hash oil, and sinsemilla. Hashish is a concentrated resinous form of cannabis that is harvested from the tops and undersides of the leaves, while hash oil is a sticky black liquid concentrate of hashish (American Psychiatric Association, 2000). Sinsemilla is high potency marijuana containing only the leaves and buds of the unpollinated female cannabis plant, where delta-9-tetrahydrocannabinol (THC) is most concentrated. THC is the key active ingredient in all cannabis and is responsible for the potency and effects of the drug (APA, 2000). The concentration of THC is determined by the growing conditions and genetic nature of the plants.

Marijuana is usually smoked as a cigarette (called a joint or nail) or in a pipe or bong (water pipes), but it can also be mixed into foods or used to brew a tea (Gahlinger, 2001). It also is smoked in blunts, which are cigars that have been emptied of tobacco and refilled with cannabis, often in combination with another drug. Marijuana smoke has a pungent and distinctive, somewhat sweet-and-sour, odor. Cannabis is produced in all 50 states, and the primary foreign sources for marijuana found in the United States are Mexico, Canada, Colombia, and Jamaica. There are countless street terms for marijuana including pot, herb, weed, grass, widow, ganja, hash, boom, Mary Jane, gangster, and chronic (Gahlinger, 2001).

Relevant History Cannabis has been used as a medicinal tonic and agent for achieving euphoria since ancient times. Its use spread from China to India and then to North Africa and Europe. In 500 B.C. the Greek historian Herodotus described a tribe of nomads who inhaled the smoke of roasted hemp seeds and became euphoric (Kaplan and Sadock, 1998). A major crop in colonial America, marijuana (hemp) was grown as a source of fiber. It was extensively cultivated during World War II, when Asian sources of hemp were cut off. In the 1960s it was used by college students and "hippies" and became a symbol of rebellion against authority. The Controlled Substances Act of 1970 classified marijuana, along with heroin and LSD, as a Schedule I drug, meaning it has the highest abuse potential and no accepted medical use (Gahlinger, 2001).

Cannabis abuse is a destructive pattern of use of the substance, leading to significant social, occupational, or medical impairment. Marijuana abuse is the proper diagnosis when at least three of the following occur: a marked increase in the amount of cannabis required to get high; greater use of the substance than intended; unsuccessful efforts to cut down or control use; increasing amounts of time spent in using, or recovering from use; important activities given up or reduced because of use; and continued use despite knowing it causes major problems (American Psychiatric Association, 2000).

Diagnostic Criteria

Rev. Kidd's investigation revealed that all forms of cannabis are psychoactive, changing how the brain works. When someone smokes marijuana, THC rapidly passes from the lungs into the bloodstream, which carries the chemical to organs throughout the body, including the brain (Kaplan and Sadock, 1998). The "high" from smoking marijuana can create a dream-like feeling of euphoria and relaxation as well as possibly bringing on paranoia, anxiety, and a panicky feeling. Short-term effects of cannabis use include problems with memory and learning, distorted perception, difficulty in thinking and problem solving, and loss of coordination. Heavy marijuana use may significantly impair normal intellectual functioning (Solowij et al., 2002).

Response to Vignette

Cannabis is the second most commonly smoked substance after tobacco. The smoke of marijuana consists of a toxic mixture of gases and particulates, many of which are known to be harmful to the lungs. A person who smokes cannabis regularly may have many of the same respiratory problems that tobacco smokers do, such as a daily cough and a heightened risk of lung infections (Tashkin, 2005). Marijuana smoking also has the potential of promoting cancer of the lungs and other parts of the respiratory tract. Cannabis users generally inhale more deeply and hold their breath longer than tobacco smokers do, which increases the lungs' exposure to smoke.

In addition, a major concern with marijuana use is the effect it has on motivation, particularly for adolescents. Chronic use interferes with normal developmental issues of youth such as educational attainment, separation from parents, forming peer relationships, and making important life choices. Even more worrying is the increasing evidence that for some adolescents heavy cannabis use can increase the chances of developing severe mental illness — psychosis or schizophrenia. The marijuana-psychosis link recently gained added credibility when a major medical journal reviewed the current research and concluded that the link was likely for some genetically predisposed youth (Fergusson et al., 2006).

Treatment within the Faith Community Substance abuse is the number one teenage mental health problem. About half of high school seniors have tried an illicit substance such as cannabis. Encouraging teens and their families to be active in the life of the community of faith is in itself a powerful preventive strategy when addressing substance abuse. Researchers have found that adolescent regular church attenders are half as likely to use marijuana as teens who do not attend church regularly (Hardert and Dowd, 1994). In Great Britain, a large study of teens found that religious belief and practice had a significant relationship to a young person's attitudes toward the impropriety of substance abuse, including the use of cannabis (Francis and Mullen, 1993). A strong youth program that promotes good communication and social skills can also be a valuable preventive measure. Teen drug abusers tend to have poor social skills, high anxiety, and low self-confidence (Sussman et al., 2000). Social skills training for adolescents can enhance coping, social problem solving, self-control, social awareness, negotiation skills, and assertiveness skills, as well as increasing the ability to resist peer pressure (Haggerty et al., 1989).

It is likely that some heavy marijuana users, like other heavy drug users, suffer from chronic anxiety, depression, or feelings of inadequacy. In these cases, the drug abuse is a symptom rather than the central problem. These individuals can benefit from referral to a mental health professional to be evaluated for psychotherapy and medication. Psychotherapy is useful when it focuses on the reasons for a person's drug abuse. In an adolescent, cannabis dependence often hides poor self-esteem, depression, severe family problems, and learning disorder issues, which will need to be addressed in therapy.

Indications for Referral

Matching treatment settings, interventions, and services to each adolescent's particular problems and needs is critical to the success of any recovery program. Because teens addicted to drugs are often uncertain about entering treatment, taking advantage of moments when they are ready to receive it is essential. Important opportunities can be lost if treatment is not immediately available.

Treatment by Mental Health Specialist

Research into adolescent addiction treatment effectiveness has examined several options, such as family therapy and group psycho-educational methods (Waldron et al., 2001) and individual behavior therapy (Diamond et al., 2002). Unfortunately the results are mixed. While research shows that these treatments reduce substance use, relapse is fairly common (Dennis et al., 2003). Addicted individuals may require prolonged treatment and multiple episodes of treatment to achieve long-term abstinence and fully restored functioning. Participation in self-help support programs during and following treatment is often helpful in maintaining abstinence.

There are several factors that appear related to adolescents being able to remain free from marijuana use after treatment. These include the degree of family cohesion, a drug-free non-violent living situation, social support from family and friends, and having friends who are not engaged in substance use and illegal activity (Babor et al., 2002). Psychological stress from family problems or the social environment make relapse more likely.

Cross-Cultural Issues   African-Americans have a higher proportion of adult treatment admissions for marijuana than other racial/ethnic groups (SAMHSA, 2005). While African-Americans are about 13 percent of the U.S. population, they make up 30 percent of adult marijuana treatment admissions. These were 76 percent male and 24 percent female, and about half were aged 18 to 24 (SAMHSA, 2005). Hispanic-Americans also make up about 13 percent of the U.S. population. That group comprises 9 percent of adult marijuana treatment admissions. European-Americans are about 70 percent of the U.S. population, while 54 percent of adult marijuana treatment admissions involve that group. Among European-Americans and Hispanic-Americans the pattern of admissions by gender and age is similar to that of African-Americans (SAMHSA, 2005).

Resources   American Academy of Child and Adolescent Psychiatry; 3615 Wisconsin Avenue, NW, Washington, DC 20016; (202) 966-7300; *www.aacap.org* deals with teen problems, including drug abuse.

American Council for Drug Education; 164 West 74th Street, New York, NY 10023; (800) 488-DRUG; *www.acde.org*.

American Psychiatric Association; 1000 Wilson Boulevard, Suite 1825, Arlington, VA 22209; (888) 35-PSYCH; *www.psych.org*.

American Psychological Association; 750 First Street, NE, Washington, DC 20002; (800) 374-2721; *www.apa.org*.

Hazelden Foundation; P.O. Box 176, Center City, MN 55012; (800) 257-7810; *www.hazelden.org*.

National Institute on Drug Abuse; National Institutes of Health, 6001 Executive Boulevard, Room 5213, Bethesda, MD 20892; (301) 443-1124; *www.drugabuse.gov*.

Helpful Books   *Cannabis Dependence: Its Nature, Consequences and Treatment* (Roger Roffman and Robert Stephens, Cambridge: Cambridge University Press, 2006).

Therapeutic Uses of Cannabis (British Medical Association, New York: Taylor and Francis, 1997).

American Psychiatric Association. (2000). *Diagnostic and statistical manual of mental disorders* (4th edition, text revision). Washington, DC: American Psychiatric Association.

Babor, T. F., Webb, C., Burleson, J. A., and Kaminer, Y. (2002). Subtypes for classifying adolescents with marijuana use disorders: Construct validity and clinical implications. *Addiction, 97,* 58–69 (Suppl. 1).

Dennis, M. L., Dawud-Noursi, S., Muck, R. D., and McDermeit (Ives), M. (2003). The need for developing and evaluating adolescent treatment models. In S. J. Stevens and A. R. Morral (Eds.), *Adolescent drug treatment in the United States: Exemplary models from a National Evaluation Study* (pp. 3–34). Binghamton, NY: Haworth Press.

Diamond, G. S., Godley, S. H., Liddle, H. A., Sampl, S., Webb, C., Tims, F. M., and Meyers, R. (2002). Five outpatient treatment models for adolescent marijuana use: A description of the Cannabis Youth Treatment interventions. *Addiction, 97,* S70–S83 (Suppl. 1).

Fergusson, D. M., Poulton, R., Smith, P. F., and Boden, J. M. (2006). Cannabis and psychosis. *British Medical Journal, 21* (332), 172–175.

Francis, L. J., and Mullen, K. (1993). Religiosity and attitudes toward drug use among 13–15 year olds in England. *Addiction, 88,* 665–672.

Gahlinger, P. M. (2001). *Illegal drugs: A complete guide to their history, chemistry, use and abuse.* Ogden, UT: Sagebrush Press.

Haggerty, K. P., Wells, E. A., Jenson, J. M., Catalano, R. F., and Hawkins, J. D. (1989). Delinquents and drug abuse: A model program for community reintegration. *Adolescence, 24,* 439–456.

Hardert, R. A., and Dowd, T. J. (1994). Alcohol and marijuana use among high school and college students in Phoenix, Arizona: A test of Kandel's socialization theory. *International Journal of Addictions, 29*(7), 887–912.

References

Kaplan, H. I., and Sadock, B. J. (1998). *Synopsis of psychiatry: Behavioral sciences/clinical psychiatry,* 8th Edition. Baltimore: Williams and Wilkins.

Nonnemaker, J. M., McNeely, C. A., and Blum, R. W. (2003). Public and private domains of religiosity and adolescent health risk behaviors: Evidence from the National Longitudinal Study of Adolescent Health. *Social Science and Medicine,* 57(11), 2049–2054.

Solowij, N., Stephens, R. S., Roffman, R. A., Babor, T., Kadden, R., Miller, M., Christiansen, K., McRee, B., and Vendetti, J. R. (2002). Marijuana Treatment Project Research Group: Cognitive functioning of long-term heavy cannabis users seeking treatment. *JAMA, 6,* 287(9), 1123–1131.

Substance Abuse and Mental Health Services Administration (SAMHSA) (2002). *The DASIS Report: Youth marijuana admissions by race and ethnicity.* Rockville, MD: Office of Applied Studies.

Substance Abuse and Mental Health Services Administration (SAMHSA) (2005). *Results from the 2004 national survey on drug use and health: National findings.* Rockville, MD: Office of Applied Studies.

Sussman, S., Dent, C. W., and Leu, L. (2000). The one-year prospective prediction of substance abuse and dependence among high-risk adolescents. *Journal of Substance Abuse,* 12(4), 373–386.

Tashkin, D. P. (2005). Smoked marijuana as a cause of lung injury. *Monaldi Archives for Chest Disease,* 63(2), 93–100.

U.S. Department of Health and Human Services. (2002). *Monitoring the Future Study.* Rockville, MD: National Institute on Drug Abuse.

Waldron, H. B., Brody, J. L., and Slesnick, N. (2001). Integrative behavioral and family therapy for adolescent substance abuse. In P. M. Monti, S. M. Colby, and T. A. O'Leary (Eds.), *Adolescents, alcohol, and substance abuse: Reaching teens through brief interventions* (pp. 216–243). New York: Guilford Press.

Methamphetamine

"He was admitted to the emergency room"

The phone call came to Pastor Paul Hanson from the community hospital. The family asked if he would come to pray and talk with the family and fifteen-year-old Adam, who had been admitted to the emergency room. The Morrison family were lifelong members of the rural Midwestern Lutheran church where Pastor Hanson had served for several years. Adam was in the bell choir and youth group. He had a history of problems at school and now the doctor at the hospital has told his parents that Adam has been using the drug methamphetamine.

Pastoral Assessment

Methamphetamine is a powerfully addictive and highly toxic stimulant that severely affects the central nervous system. There is increasing evidence that it has lasting adverse impact on the brain (Cho and Melega, 2002). It increases energy and alertness and decreases appetite. Methamphetamine, like cocaine, results in an accumulation of the neurotransmitter dopamine, and this elevated dopamine concentration produces feelings of euphoria in the user (Cho and Melega, 2002).

Methamphetamine can be smoked, snorted, orally ingested, or injected. Smokable methamphetamine, known as "ice," looks like glass slivers or clear rock salt and became a popular way to use the drug during the 1980s (Gahlinger, 2001). Smoking methamphetamine is probably the most toxic form of ingestion; in addition to damaging effects on teeth, it is very injurous to the lungs. As crack is to cocaine, ice is to methamphetamine, potent and dangerous.

When a user smokes or injects methamphetamine, an intense euphoric rush is felt, almost at once (Gahlinger, 2001). Snorting the substance affects the user in about 5 minutes, while oral ingestion takes about 20 minutes for the effects to be felt. The intense rush and exhilaration from the drug results from the release of high levels of dopamine into the section of the brain that controls the feeling of pleasure. The effects of methamphetamine can last up to 12 hours.

Relevant History   Amphetamine, from which methamphetamine is derived, was first synthesized in Germany in 1887 (Gahlinger, 2001). Little was done with the drug until the late 1920s, when it began to be examined as a treatment for a variety of illnesses. In 1937 amphetamine was found to have a positive effect on some children with attention deficit hyperactivity disorder (ADHD). Persons with ADHD have difficulty concentrating. When given amphetamine, some people with ADHD notably improve their concentration and performance. Instead of making ADHD sufferers more jumpy, as might be expected, amphetamine calms them down. During World War II, amphetamines were widely used to keep soldiers alert (Gahlinger, 2001).

Methamphetamine is more potent and easier to make than amphetamine. It was discovered by a pharmacist in Japan in 1919 (Gahlinger, 2001). In the United States in the 1950s, legally manufactured tablets of both dextroamphetamine (Dexedrine) and methamphetamine (Methedrine) became available and were used by college students, truck drivers, and athletes. The 1960s saw the start of the significant use of clandestine labs to make methamphetamine (Gahlinger, 2001). Over the last decade rural areas of the United States have had a great increase in methamphetamine use.

Addiction to methamphetamine is a chronic, relapse-prone disease, characterized by compulsive drug-seeking and drug use (American Psychiatric Association, 2000). Frequent use of methamphetamine brings a tolerance for the drug. As the body adapts to the substance, an individual needs larger doses to achieve the same result. As a consequence, users will try to intensify the desired effect by taking increasing amounts of the drug, using it more often, or changing their method of intake. Some abusers will not eat or sleep for days during a binge, also termed a "run." Methamphetamine use can cause agitation, anxiety, headache, blurred vision, dizziness, insomnia, stomach cramps, and shaking (Rawson et al., 2002).

Diagnostic Criteria

Continued methamphetamine abuse can lead to psychotic behavior, including severe paranoia, visual and auditory hallucinations, and out-of-control rages that can result in violent incidents (APA, 2000). Chronic abusers at times develop sores on their bodies from scratching at "crank bugs," the common delusion that bugs are crawling under the skin. Methamphetamine use can also bring on aggressive behavior and violence, and there are increasing numbers of cases seen in emergency rooms (Maxwell, 2005).

Other serious side effects include convulsions, dangerously high body temperature, stroke, memory loss, neurological damage, cardiac arrhythmia, and death. When methamphetamine abuse ends, several withdrawal symptoms can arise, including depression, anxiety, fatigue, paranoia, and an intense craving for the drug. Psychotic symptoms sometimes persist for months or years after use has ceased. In animal studies researchers have found that significant numbers of the dopamine-producing cells in the brain that generate pleasure can be damaged after prolonged exposure to methamphetamine (Segal et al., 2005).

Methamphetamine is widely available throughout the United Sates. It can be easily and relatively inexpensively manufactured in clandestine laboratories using ingredients that can be purchased in local stores (Santos et al., 2005). Over-the-counter cold medicines containing ephedrine or pseudoephedrine and other materials are "cooked" in "meth labs" to make the preparation. These chemical mixtures create highly dangerous concoctions and their by-products are extremely toxic (Santos et al., 2005). Disposal of a methamphetamine lab requires professionals specially trained in hazardous materials management. It is estimated that for every pound of methamphetamine produced, five pounds of hazardous waste are also created.

These labs can be portable and are easily moved to avoid law enforcement detection. "Meth labs" have been built in many types of locations, including apartments, hotel rooms, rented storage spaces, and trucks (Santos et al., 2005). These factors make methamphetamine a drug with a high potential for widespread abuse. Street terms for methamphetamine include: blue meth, chicken feed, cinnamon, crink, crystal meth, desocsins, geep, granulated orange, hot ice, ice, kaksonjae, L.A. glass, lemon drop, meth, OZs, peanut butter, sketch, spoosh, stove top, super ice, tick tick, trash, wash, working man's cocaine, yellow barn, and yellow powder (Gahlinger, 2001).

Response to Vignette

Pastor Hanson was able to guide the family through the crisis by being supportive as well as by providing accurate information about the drug and its possible effects. Mercifully, Adam had only been experimenting with "meth" for a short time, so the risk of permanent brain impairment was lessened. Adam had been frightened by his physical reaction to the drug, which caused severe agitation, anxiety, and heart palpitations, and prompted him to go to the emergency room. He thought that he was having a heart attack.

He was motivated to enter treatment, which began with a complete assessment by the hospital psychologist which revealed that Adam had signs of clinical depression. A stimulant like methamphetamine is often used as a form of self-medication for an untreated depression. If the underlying depression is addressed with appropriate medication and psychotherapy, the need for the illegal and dangerous substances may be removed. Psychological testing also revealed that Adam had a learning problem that could account for some of his difficulties in school and needed to be addressed.

It is important that the faith community be informed about the negative effects and growing problem of methamphetamine abuse. Since 1990, methamphetamine use has risen noticeably, chiefly in the western United States (National Institute on Drug Abuse, 2000). Most users are European-American males between 19 and 24 years of age. According to the U.S. Department of Health and Human Services 2002 report, more than 12 million people age 12 and older (5.3 percent) reported that they had used methamphetamine at least once in their lifetime and 0.3 percent reported use in the past month. In the University of Michigan's *Monitoring the Future* 2002 survey, annual methamphetamine use ranged from 2.2 percent among 8th graders, to 3.9 percent among 10th graders, to 3.6 percent among 12th graders, 1.2 percent for college students, and 2.5 percent for young adults (U.S. Department of Health and Human Services, 2002).

Treatment within the Faith Community

Effective prevention programs to address this problem should start early for youngsters. Youth need to be provided with comprehensive knowledge of the dangers involved in the use of the substance. Family-focused prevention efforts have been found to have a greater effect than strategies that focus on parents only or youth only. The faith community is an ideal place for the development of educational and preventive programs to counter the growing use of this dangerous substance.

Clergy, especially in rural areas, need to develop a working relationship with at least one mental health professional who has a comprehensive knowledge of mental health services for addictions in the region. Pastors need such a professional with whom they can confer to make an assessment of the issues and to whom they can make a referral. Because of a shortage of mental health professionals in rural areas, clergy may need to be more creative in finding mental health colleagues

Indications for Referral

than their urban counterparts. This may mean finding a consultant who can be reached by phone or Internet prior to a crisis situation. Rural hospitals may be the first place to consider linkage since most non-urban psychologists and psychiatrists tend to be concentrated in hospital settings (Human and Wasem, 1991).

Treatment by Mental Health Specialist

There are no pharmacological treatments available for methamphetamine dependence, although antidepressants are frequently used to address the depressive symptoms associated with withdrawal (Grabowski et al., 2004). The most successful treatment for methamphetamine addiction is cognitive behavioral intervention, which works to change a person's thinking and behavior. This method of therapy also seeks to increase coping skills to deal with life stressors. Methamphetamine recovery support groups are an effective therapy strategy for many people seeking recovery (Rawson et al., 2002).

Relapse prevention should be a part of any methamphetamine treatment program. It is a means to help abusers cope more effectively by seeking to recognize and overcome the stressors or "triggers" in their environment that may cause relapse. Drug addiction when left untreated or poorly treated often results in persistent relapse.

Persons recovering from methamphetamine addiction often suffer from depression and severe low self-esteem due to chemical withdrawal (Richman et al., 2002) and the memory of negative events that transpired during addiction. In order to deal with those memories, an individual may return to drug abuse. Relapse prevention programs help persons begin to build back their self-esteem and learn to live with painful memories.

Cross-Cultural Issues

The use of methamphetamine and other amphetamines has become a major problem in several parts of the globe, with the greatest use in Asia. According to the United Nations, 30 million people abuse these substances, as compared to 15 million who use opiates and 13 million who use cocaine. The highest rates of use are in Thailand, Australia, New Zealand, and the Philippines (Maxwell, 2005).

American Academy of Addiction Psychiatry; 1010 Vermont Avenue, NW, Suite 710, Washington, DC 20005; (202) 393-4484; *www.aaap .org.*

American Academy of Child and Adolescent Psychiatry has a website with free information on teen problems, including drug abuse, at *www.aacap.org.*

American Society of Addiction Medicine; 4601 North Park Avenue, Upper Arcade #101, Chevy Chase, MD 20815; (301) 656-3920; *www.asam.org*; is a medical society dedicated to educating physicians and improving the treatment of individuals suffering from alcoholism and other addictions.

Crystal Meth Anonymous; 8205 Santa Monica Blvd., PMB 1–114, West Hollywood, CA 90046; (213) 488-4455 (hot line); *www.crystalmeth .org*; is a 12-step fellowship for those in recovery from addiction to crystal meth. There are no dues or fees for membership, which is open to anyone with a desire to stop using.

Haight Ashbury Free Clinics; P.O. Box 29917, San Francisco, CA 94129; (415) 522-2114; *www.hafci.org*; serve more than 65,000 individuals and their loved ones every year. They provide free, high-quality health care that is culturally sensitive, nonjudgmental, and accessible to all in need.

Hazelden Foundation; P.O. Box 176, Center City, MN 55012; (800) 257-7810; *www.hazelden.org.*

National Clearinghouse for Alcohol and Drug Information; P.O. Box 2345, Rockville, MD 20847; (800) 729-6686; *www.health.org*; provides free, useful materials about the many aspects of adolescent alcohol and drug abuse treatment and prevention. Several of these publications are designed for the faith community.

National Institute on Drug Abuse; National Institutes of Health, 6001 Executive Boulevard, Room 5213, Bethesda, MD 20892-9561; (301) 443-1124; *www.drugabuse.gov.*

Safe and Drug-Free Schools; Office of Elementary and Secondary Education, U.S. Department of Education, 600 Independence Avenue, SW, Washington, DC 20202-0498; (800) 624-0100; *www.ed.gov/about/offices/list/oese;* is the federal government's principal program for reducing drug use and violence, through education and prevention activities in our nation's schools.

Helpful Books

The Official Patient's Sourcebook on Methamphetamine Dependence: A Revised and Updated Directory for the Internet Age (Icon Health, San Diego, CA: Icon Health Publications, 2002).

Speed and Methamphetamine Drug Dangers (Mary Ann Littell, Berkeley Heights, NJ: Enslow Publishers, 2004).

Straight Talk from Claudia Black: What Recovering Parents Should Tell Their Kids about Drugs and Alcohol (Claudia Black, Minneapolis, MN: Hazelden Publishing and Educational Services, 2003).

References

American Psychiatric Association. (2000). *Diagnostic and statistical manual of mental disorders* (4th edition, text revision). Washington, DC: American Psychiatric Association.

Cho, A. K., and Melega, W. P. (2002). Patterns of methamphetamine abuse and their consequences. *Journal of Addictive Diseases,* 21(1), 21–34.

Gahlinger, P. M. (2001). *Illegal drugs: A complete guide to their history, chemistry, use and abuse.* Ogden, UT: Sagebrush Press.

Grabowski, J., Shearer, J., Merrill, J., and Negus, S. S. (2004). Agonist-like, replacement pharmacotherapy for stimulant abuse and dependence. *Addictive Behavior,* 29(7), 1439–1464.

Human, J., and Wasem, C. (1991). Rural mental health in America. *American Psychologist,* 46(3), 232–239.

Maxwell, J. C. (2005). Emerging research on methamphetamine. *Current Opinion in Psychiatry,* 18(3), 235–242.

National Institute on Drug Abuse. (2000). *Epidemiologic trends in drug abuse advance report, December 2000: Community Epidemiology Work Group.* Rockville, MD: U.S. Department of Health and Human Services.

Rawson, R. A., Gonzales, R., and Brethen, P. (2002). Treatment of methamphetamine use disorders: An update. *Journal of Substance Abuse Treatment,* 23(2), 145–150.

Richman, K. S., Iguchi, M. Y., and Anglin, M. D. (2002). Depressive symptoms among amphetamine and cocaine users before and after substance abuse treatment. *Psychology of Addictive Behaviors,* 16(4), 333–337.

Santos, A. P., Wilson, A. K., Hornung, C. A., Polk, H. C., Rodriguez, J. L., and Franklin, G. A. (2005). Methamphetamine laboratory explosions: A new and emerging burn injury. *Journal of Burn Care and Rehabilitation,* 26(3), 228–232.

Segal, D. S., Kuczenski, R., O'Neil, M. L., Melega, W. P., and Cho, A. K. (2005). Prolonged exposure of rats to intravenous methamphetamine: Behavioral and neurochemical characterization. *Psychopharmacology,* 180(3), 501–512.

U.S. Department of Health and Human Services. (2002). *Monitoring the Future Study.* Rockville, MD: National Institute on Drug Abuse.

Over-the-Counter Drug Abuse

"I'm having trouble sleeping"

Sarah is a 65-year-old married woman who has attended Pastor Tom's church with her husband, Bill, for many years. For the past couple of weeks, Bill has been alone at services. Concerned, Pastor Tom asks him about Sarah. Bill responds, "Actually, I'm really worried about her. Recently she's been more and more disoriented, forgetting important appointments and scared to leave the house. She's having trouble sleeping and at times feels dizzy. I'm afraid she might have Alzheimer's disease. She won't see the doctor, though. I think she's scared about what might be wrong with her."

Pastor Tom asked, "Would it be helpful if I made a visit to your house?" Bill quickly accepted the offer, "That would be wonderful. I hope you can convince her to see a doctor."

When Pastor Tom arrived at their home, Bill answered the door, "Thanks for coming. Sarah is in the kitchen." She greeted their guest, "Bill told me you were coming. I hope he didn't alarm you. Really, I'm fine." Sarah did not look fine, however. She seemed a bit disoriented and uncertain, as if having trouble recognizing who had come to visit. "Have a seat," she said hesitatingly and slowly turned back to the kitchen sink, making an effort to act as if everything were normal. Pastor Tom responded, "Sarah, it's good to see you. How have you been doing?" With her back to him, Sarah said, "Pretty good, considering. I've been having trouble sleeping at night. That can affect my whole day." The pastor asked, "How long have you been having problems sleeping?" "A long time," responded Sarah. "I can't remember when it started. I'm having trouble remembering things, too. It's really no big deal, though. Probably from lack of sleep and this cold I've had for the past couple of weeks." Carefully, he asked, "Have you gone to see a doctor about it?" "No, it's not bad enough for that. This medicine I bought at the supermarket helps me a lot," she said, pointing to a bottle on the kitchen table.

Bill interjected, "I think that medicine is causing the problem. I've noticed that you take two of those pills before you go to bed, and I think you take them again when you wake up a couple hours later, don't you?" Defensively, Sarah replies, "Don't start on that again. Those pills work for only a couple of hours, and I need my sleep." He responded, "If it were only the pills, I wouldn't be worried. I'm afraid you're taking too much of that cold medicine, too. I think all these medicines might be interacting with each other or something."

Pastoral Assessment Pastor Tom's first task was to carefully evaluate Sarah. She looked groggy, was a bit disoriented, and was not acting right. He had known her for a long time, and she sounded and looked different from usual. Her level of alertness seemed to be waxing and waning. But Sarah did not seem to recognize this and minimized the problem. She tried to remain friendly, but seemed frustrated and was having difficulty following the conversation. Sarah looked like she was drugged.

Bill confirmed that Sarah had a long history of problems with sleeping and recently had been fighting off a cold. However, she had only been acting strangely for the past two weeks, since "she's been taking all that stuff from the grocery store." She had resisted efforts to take her to see the doctor.

At this point, Pastor Tom needed more information, so he took Bill aside and inquired further. "What other kinds of medical problems does Sarah have?" Bill told him that she has high blood pressure and has been taking a pill the doctor prescribed for that. She has been having problems with incontinence, sometimes wetting herself, which has seriously embarrassed her. In fact, when she saw the doctor several months ago, he prescribed a medication to calm her bladder called oxybutinin (Ditropan). That seems to be working well and she has not lost bladder control since starting on it, but she has begun complaining about constipation.

The pastor asked Bill if she was taking any other medication besides the prescriptions, such as over-the-counter (OTC) drugs. He explained that the only other medication she takes is the pills to help her sleep (Tylenol PM) and the NyQuil for her cold.

Next, he asked if Sarah has a history of psychological problems or problems with alcohol or other drugs. Bill says that she used to drink pretty heavily and still has a couple of glasses of wine with supper and sometimes a glass before she goes to bed.

Relevant History

Sarah has not been feeling well for at least a month, and things have gotten worse over the past two weeks. She has become progressively more forgetful, groggy, and behaves in an unusual manner. She also has a history of heavy alcohol use and is currently drinking two or three glasses of wine each evening. Sarah is having trouble sleeping and is taking an OTC sleeping aid. She has also been self-medicating her cold. On top of all this, she takes two prescription medications. Despite these ongoing problems, she has been reluctant to see her doctor and keeps using more and more OTC medications that temporarily relieve her symptoms.

Diagnostic Criteria

Sarah is likely experiencing a delirium caused by *over-the-counter drug abuse* and may have unknowingly relapsed into alcohol abuse/misuse as well. Delirium is indicated by the relatively recent onset of fluctuating levels of alertness, memory difficulties, disorientation, and dizziness, given no prior history of such problems (American Psychiatric Association, 2000). There are specific organic substances that are likely responsible for her problems — the OTC medications she is taking and at least one of her prescription medications. However, other more serious conditions need to be ruled out in a 65-year-old woman.

Sarah has high blood pressure, which could predispose her to having a stroke. A stroke could cause confusion, and multiple small strokes could also cause memory impairment. She may also be in the early stages of Alzheimer's disease, although this is unlikely because of the rapid development of memory difficulties and her relatively young age. The dizziness may be due to low blood pressure caused by too high a dose of blood pressure medication. Sarah could also have a bladder infection that has spread into her blood stream, causing a delirium that will require immediate medical attention and treatment with antibiotics.

After leaving Bill and Sarah's home, Pastor Tom looks on the Internet for information about the prescription and OTC drugs that Sarah is taking. He learns that Sarah's symptoms might actually be explained by interactions between her prescription drugs, the OTC medications that she is using, and her alcohol intake. Tylenol PM, an OTC drug used for sleep, is a combination of acetaminophen and diphenhydramine (Benadryl). NyQuil, a commonly used cold medicine, is a combination of doxylamine succinate (an antihistamine like diphenhydramine) and acetaminophen, and is 10 percent alcohol by volume (similar to wine). In summary, Sarah is taking three drugs that all have "anticholinergic" side effects (oxybutinin, diphenhydramine, and doxylamine succinate), which include dizziness, constipation, and, especially, trouble with memory and concentration. Sarah may have an anticholinergic delirium induced by these three drugs (American Psychiatric Association, 2000).

With further reading on the subject, Pastor Tom was amazed to learn how many older adults take OTC drugs to treat physical or emotional symptoms. Some studies report that 31–87 percent of the elderly take OTC medications. Almost 80 percent of persons taking OTC drugs also use alcohol, prescribed drugs, or both. OTC drugs are most often taken to relieve arthritis, difficulty with sleep, or problems with constipation (Stoehr et al., 1997). Other predictors of OTC use by seniors include low income, trouble with mobility, and difficulty getting to doctors (Amoako et al., 2003). The following OTC drugs are those most commonly abused by persons over age 65:

1. Pain relievers such as aspirin or non-steroidal anti-inflammatory drugs, which can cause stomach ulcers, gastritis, liver or kidney damage, or increased blood pressure

2. Laxatives, which can cause diarrhea, dehydration, changes in the salt content of the blood, or chronic constipation as the bowel becomes dependent on the laxative

3. Cold preparations containing antihistamines (such as diphenhydramine and doxylamine succinate) and decongestants (such as phenylpropanolamine and pseudoephedrine) which can cause disorientation and memory problems, dizziness, falls, visual hallucinations, high blood pressure, heart arrhythmias, or chronic sinus congestion

4. Alcohol-containing medications, which can cause a relapse into alcoholism, liver damage if taken in large enough amounts for a long enough period, over-sedation, inattentiveness, or falls

5. Caffeine-containing drugs, as seen with certain combination pain relievers, which can cause tremors, anxiety, insomnia, or heart arrhythmias

6. Many kinds of alternative medicine preparations, including megavitamins and a host of herbal preparations, which may cause over-sedation, insomnia, memory impairment, severe sunburn, and may interact with prescription medications (Hanlon et al., 2001).

OTC drugs are a lot more dangerous than most people think. As individuals age, their bodies and nervous systems do not have as much flexibility as they did when they were in their thirties, forties, or fifties, especially if a person is already taking prescription drugs that may impair liver and kidney function (the major systems that rid the body of ingested drugs).

Response to Vignette

Asking Bill about his wife was the first step to beginning a dialogue with him about a possible problem with Sarah. The pastor then offered to visit, which allowed him to collect further information about the situation. Particularly important was Pastor Tom's inquiry about prescription or OTC drugs that Sarah was taking, and then looking up some of the side-effects of these medications. This information gathering helped him to decide what to do next.

Pastor Tom should now strongly encourage Bill to take Sarah to see a medical doctor, whether she agrees or not. The pastor might even offer to accompany them to the physician and support Bill in his reasons for insisting that Sarah go. Pastor Tom should also be sure that Bill brings all of Sarah's prescription *and especially* non-prescription OTC drugs to the doctor's office. It would also be helpful if Bill wrote out the name, dose, and frequency that Sarah takes each of the medications and gave the list to the doctor.

Treatment within the Faith Community

There are limitations as to how actively involved the faith community can be in Sarah's OTC abuse problem. The pastor, church staff, and friends can help to monitor Sarah's condition by noticing when she has been absent and then asking Bill about this, as the pastor did. The church can support Bill in the actions that he must take to have Sarah evaluated, and then help the couple comply with whatever treatment program the doctor prescribes (if they need help).

The faith community is ideally positioned to keep an eye on elderly members for changes in their behavior or activities that suggest a problem, contacting them to obtain more information, and then supporting them in resolving the problem. If older members are so ill that they are homebound or otherwise cannot participate, regular phone calls or in-person visits can be made to check on them. Older adults after the loss of a spouse or the onset of major medical problems can quickly become isolated, lonely, and depressed, and may begin to neglect themselves.

For members to effectively monitor older persons in the congregation, they must first be adequately informed about the signs and symptoms of common conditions in later life (including OTC drug abuse) that signal a health problem. Second, the congregation can help to support the spouse or other family members who are trying to care for a person. This can take many forms, including simply being a friend and offering a listening ear. At times it also may include being pro-active in pointing out a problem, encouraging active problem solving, and helping a family member carry out needed solutions.

Bear in mind, however, that actions taken by the faith community in making recommendations or even being supportive must not be done in an intrusive, insensitive manner. Such actions are permissible only after explicit and full permission from the older person and his or her family is obtained, unless that person's safety or health is imminently in danger.

Indications for Referral

When a pastor or other member of the faith community believes that OTC drug abuse may be present, an immediate referral to an appropriately trained physician is indicated. This is especially true when delirium could be present, given the dangers to safety that this involves; delirium is associated with a high mortality rate in older persons.

Treatment by Mental Health Specialist

Sarah's doctor should conduct a complete physical examination, neurological evaluation, and mental status testing (asking questions about memory and orientation), obtain blood tests, and carefully review all of the prescription and OTC drugs that she is taking. The physician will probably order a urinalysis and possibly a urine culture if the urinalysis is abnormal, since a bladder infection can lead to disorientation and memory problems like Sarah is having.

During the visit, the doctor should explain the dangers and risks of the prescription and OTC medications that Sarah is taking and strongly recommend that the drugs contributing to her problem be stopped unless they are essential for other health reasons. The physician should be explicit about this in order to break through the minimization or denial that Sarah may exhibit to justify her continued use of these substances. All of this should be done with Bill in the room so that he can be sure that Sarah complies.

Cross-Cultural Issues Almost every culture has folk remedies for the treatment of common health problems. Not all of these remedies are safe and some could make the problem worse, especially when taken in large quantities or over a long period of time. If there is any question about the contents of a particular home remedy, its contents can be analyzed by a toxicology lab at a hospital emergency room.

Resources Information about OTC drugs can be obtained by a telephone call to a local emergency room, pharmacist, or poison control center. In this way, updated information can be obtained on the side-effects of OTC drugs and on their interactions with prescription medications.

Most university medical centers have a drug information service that can be accessed by anyone in the country by simply calling the medical center's main number and asking for this service or for their poison control center. The following U.S. Department of Health and Human Services website contains specific information on OTC drugs that are often abused: *www.health.org/nongovpubs/prescription*. A similar website operated by the American Society of Anesthesiologists with even more details on OTC drug abuse is *www.asahq.org/news/factsheet.htm*.

American Academy for Addiction Psychiatry; 1010 Vermont Avenue, NW, Suite 710, Washington, DC 20005; (202) 393-4484; *www.aaap .org*.

American Academy for Geriatric Psychiatry; 7910 Woodmont Avenue, Suite 1050, Bethesda, MD 20814-3004; (301) 654-7850; *www .aagponline.org*.

American Psychiatric Association; 1000 Wilson Boulevard, Suite 1825, Arlington, VA 22209; (703) 907-7300; *www.psych.org*.

American Society of Addiction Medicine; 4601 North Park Avenue, Upper Arcade #101, Chevy Chase, MD 20815; (301) 656-3920; *www.asam.org*; is a medical society dedicated to educating physicians and improving the treatment of individuals suffering from addictions.

National Institute on Drug Abuse; National Institutes of Health, 6001 Executive Boulevard, Bethesda, MD 20852; (301) 443-1124; *www.drugabuse.gov*.

Helpful Books

Over-the-Counter Drugs: Harmless or Hazardous? (Paul R. Sanberg, New York: Chelsea House, 1988).

Pharmacists Guide to the Most Misused and Abused Drugs in America: Prescription Drugs, Over the Counter Drugs, Street Drugs, and Designer Drugs (Ken Liska, New York: Collier, 1988).

Swallowing a Bitter Pill: How Prescription and Over-the-Counter Drug Abuse Is Ruining Lives — My Story (Cindy R. Mogil, Far Hills, NJ: New Horizon Press, 2001).

References

American Psychiatric Association. (2000). *Diagnostic and statistical manual of mental disorders* (4th edition, text revision). Washington, DC: American Psychiatric Association.

Amoako, E. P., Richardson-Campbell, L., and Kennedy-Malone, L. (2003). Self-medication with over-the-counter drugs among elderly adults. *Journal of Gerontological Nursing,* 29(8), 10–15.

Hanlon, J. T., Fillenbaum, G. G., Ruby, C. M., Gray, S., and Bohannon, A. (2001). Epidemiology of over-the-counter drug use in community dwelling elderly: United States perspective. *Drugs and Aging,* 18(2), 123–131.

Stoehr, G. P., Ganguli, M., Seaberg, E. C., Echement, D. A., and Belle, S. (1997). Over-the-counter medication use in an older rural community: The MOVIES Project. *Journal of the American Geriatrics Society, 45*(2), 158–165.

Overeating

"Weight reduction programs in churches have positive benefits"

Rev. Ben Culp had been pastor at a medium-sized primarily African-American congregation for five years when Dr. Ann Love, an active member, came to him with the idea of developing a weight reduction program for overweight persons in the church. She was a professor of nursing at the university and had spoken with friends at a church in another city that had had success with such a group. Rev. Culp, Dr. Love, and several other members formed a study group to examine the research on weight reduction programs in church settings and the needs in their congregation. They discovered solid evidence that health promotion programs in churches, including those for weight loss, have shown positive benefits for members and that such programs are often highly desired and greatly needed.

Pastoral Assessment

Rev. Culp, Professor Love, and the exploratory committee reported their findings to the church council and recommended organizing a weight reduction program based upon their assessment of the scientific research and the needs of members. They concluded that a church-based effort focused on weight reduction and good nutrition could potentially minister to a substantial group of people who might not otherwise seek support or assistance.

Among the information they reviewed was a study of 117 randomly selected members in five urban African-American congregations in Chicago. The researchers found that more than two in three congregants interviewed expressed specific concerns regarding their weight, diet, and exercise practices, and these were the most frequent health concerns in the group (Baldwin et al., 2001). Younger adults were much more concerned about all aspects of their health than older members. Females were considerably more likely to express worry about health habits and health risks than males. It was troubling that no significant relationship was found between articulated health needs and access to care among congregation members (Baldwin et al., 2001).

Several types of health promotion programs have proven to be successful in church settings, including cancer screening, blood pressure control, diabetes education, stroke prevention, smoking cessation, cholesterol education, and weight reduction (Yanek et al., 2001). Congregations are places where information can be exchanged through established social networks in settings like weekly services and regular meetings. Churches also offer an array of support resources, such as peer counseling and pastoral care. Because the black church is an institution in which African-Americans have trust and long-term commitments, such programs may have an increased likelihood of successful outcomes (Sbrocco et al., 2005).

Relevant History   African-Americans, particularly women, have a disproportionately high rate of overweight and obesity (extreme overweight) compared with the general population. Among African-American women 69 percent are overweight, and poor women in general are 50 percent more likely to be overweight than those in the highest income levels (Klauer and Aronne, 2002). Overweight is associated with negative body image in both genders, although more so among women than men (Klauer and Aronne, 2002). It has been documented that overweight individuals face prejudice and discrimination when seeking college admissions, employment, and even a place to live (Wadden et al., 2002). African-American women who can benefit from weight loss may be less likely to attempt it and may have relatively less success in using traditional weight loss programs compared to their European-American counterparts (Davis et al., 1999).

Obesity is also a serious health problem for the nation's children and adolescents. One of five children and teenagers is overweight. The occurrence of adolescent obesity has more than doubled over the last three decades (Troiano et al., 1995). Being seriously overweight in adolescence dramatically increases the risk of adult obesity. This is alarming because being overweight is considered a major public health threat directly linked to a number of disabling and life-threatening diseases (Khaodhiar and Blackburn, 2002). Central to reducing the problem is the need to change public understanding of obesity from seeing it as an issue of appearance to a disease that can be prevented, treated, and successfully managed.

Diagnostic Criteria

Obesity develops as a result of a complex interaction between a person's lifestyle, environment, cultural influences, and genetic makeup (Khaodhiar and Blackburn, 2002). In contemporary American culture, while consumption of high caloric foods has steadily increased, physical activity has appreciably decreased. A great many persons are overweight as a result of small weight gains over an extended period of time (Khaodhiar and Blackburn, 2002).

The number of adults in the United States and other wealthy nations who are either somewhat overweight or obese is growing at a disquieting rate (National Center for Health Statistics, 2000). During the decade of the 1990s the rate of obesity among U.S. adults increased 1 percent each year (Klauer and Aronne, 2002). Of the estimated 97 million adults in the United States who are overweight, 44.3 million are obese. These individuals face greater risk for developing coronary heart disease, hypertension, stroke, gall bladder disease, and Type 2 diabetes mellitus than those at normal weight (Aronne, 2001). Researchers have also found a strong relationship between being overweight and death rates from cancer (Calle et al., 2003).

The increasing frequency of obesity and its associated complications places an enormous burden on health care use and costs. In addition to the more than $100 billion in medical costs associated with being overweight, Americans also spend an estimated $38 billion each year on weight loss programs and products (Spence-Jones, 2003). At any given time, about 44 percent of women and 29 percent of men in the United States are attempting to lose weight (Serdula et al., 1999).

Weight reduction can best be achieved through dietary intervention and behavioral or "lifestyle" changes, while weight maintenance is furthered through increased physical activity (Pronk and Wing, 1994). Poor maintenance of treatment-directed weight loss remains a major challenge in the management of obesity. The rate of physical activity is the most reliable predictor of long-term weight reduction maintenance. Those who consistently have the highest rates of exercise are the individuals who are most likely to sustain their weight loss (Pronk and Wing, 1994). "Quick fixes" do not offer long-term results when addressing weight reduction. The good news is that even small losses (5 to 10 percent of body weight) can have health benefits (Klauer and Aronne, 2002).

Response to Vignette   Rev. Culp's church accepted the challenge of developing a weight reduction group as recommended by the exploratory committee that reviewed the scientific findings (Yanek et al., 2001). Dr. Love and her colleagues at the nursing school provided a basic health screening for all those who wished to participate in the program. The church used a standard behavioral group program addressing nutrition and physical activity, along with a strong spiritual component that was culturally integrated for African-American churchgoers. For example, the group incorporated prayers and health messages employing appropriate biblical passages. Physical activities included group aerobics done to gospel music and praise songs. Rev. Culp regularly shared healthy eating and exercise information in his weekly e-mail newsletter to church members and often praised the program from the pulpit. At 6 and 12 months there were additional health screenings, which found that participants achieved clinically important improvements in their health. This church-based intervention had significant benefit for many who participated.

Churches are the largest social, voluntary, spiritual, and educational institutions in African-American communities. Researchers have consistently found that religion plays an important role in the lives of African-Americans and that the church often contributes to their well-being and social support (Levin et al., 2005). Religion and spirituality are associated with health-seeking behaviors for African-Americans, particularly women. In a 2001 national survey of 812 African-American women, 43 percent reported using religion/spirituality for health reasons in the past year (Dessio et al., 2004). **Treatment within the Faith Community**

One of the most important areas of emerging research in health and religion is that of health promotion in congregations. Kumanyika and Charleson (1992) at Pennsylvania State University found that weight loss, as well as related dietary and behavioral changes resulting from participation in a church-based weight control program, significantly enhances blood pressure control among African-American women. In this study, the support for dieting and exercise was provided in the congregation, with all participants sharing a common belief system.

The church members were committed to helping each other succeed based upon their religious beliefs — the crucial factor in the program — as the study's authors acknowledge: "The built-in support system within the church is viewed as a key to the program. Through church activities such as choir rehearsal, prayer night, and Sunday services, weight control program participants in the church setting know each other and are in frequent contact with each other outside of the weight control classes. This provides a natural environment for mutual support and reinforcement" (Kumanyika and Charleson, 1992, p. 23).

Indications for Referral Health promotion programs need to begin with a basic health status screening as was done here. Some individuals in these screenings may demonstrate a need to be referred for further medical attention. For example, someone who shows signs of higher than normal blood pressure will need a referral to a physician who can help the person manage the hypertension.

Treatment by Mental Health Specialist Although obese individuals report feeling guilty and ashamed about being overweight, there is no hard evidence that overweight persons have more psychological problems than those at average weight (Bartlett et al., 1996). Nevertheless, some individuals struggling with overeating may need counseling to address psychological issues, such as depression and anxiety.

For a few very obese people, surgery is a viable option that can bring long-term weight loss. Medical operations for weight loss are called bariatric surgeries (Fobi, 2004), of which gastric bypass is the most common. In this treatment the size of the stomach is reduced considerably. The procedure limits how much a person can eat at one time and greatly restricts the body's ability to absorb nutrients and calories. Because there can be complications, this surgery should be performed only when all else has been unsuccessful. The weight loss from such a procedure can result in marked improvements and, in some cases, complete resolution of the medical conditions associated with obesity. Persons undergoing surgery for obesity need lifelong nutritional supplements and medical monitoring (Fobi, 2004).

Cross-Cultural Issues Survey findings indicate that European-Americans consume more high-fiber cereals and fruits than do African-Americans, and they consume more whole grains as a cancer prevention strategy (Cotugna et al., 1992). Although African-Americans eat more green and leafy vegetables than do European-Americans, they also eat more high-fat items, such as fried food and processed meats (Borrud et al., 1989). The frequency of obesity, especially in African-American women, may in part be a consequence of ethnic differences in eating patterns and is a noteworthy health risk for African-Americans.

American Dietetic Association; 120 South Riverside Plaza, Suite 2000, Chicago, IL 60606; (800) 877-1600; *www.eatright.org*; founded in 1917, this is the nation's largest organization of food and nutrition professionals.

American Obesity Association (AOA); 1250 24th Street, NW, Suite 300, Washington, DC 20037; (202) 776-7711; *www.obesity.org*; focuses on changing public policy and perceptions about obesity. AOA is seeking to change the attitude that obesity represents personal failure to an understanding of it as a complex disease involving environmental and genetic issues.

International Obesity Task Force; 231 North Gower Street, London NW1 2NR, United Kingdom; 44 (0) 20.7691.1900; *www.iotf.org*; a global network working with the World Health Organization to alert people to the growing health crisis caused by increasing levels of obesity.

National Heart, Lung, and Blood Institute of the National Institutes of Health formed the Obesity Education Initiative; NHLBI Health Information Center, P.O. Box 30105, Bethesda, MD 20824; (301) 592-8573; *www.nhlbi.nih.gov*. The overall purpose of the initiative is to help reduce the incidence of overweight in order to reduce the risk of coronary heart disease and overall mortality.

NAASO, The Obesity Society; 8630 Fenton Street, Suite 918, Silver Spring, MD 20910; (301) 563-6526; *www.naaso.org*; promotes research, education, and advocacy to better understand, prevent, and treat obesity.

Rudd Center for Food Policy and Obesity; 309 Edwards Street, Yale University, New Haven, CT 06520; (203) 432-6700; *www .yaleruddcenter.org*; has the mission to document, understand, and ameliorate the bias, stigma, and discrimination associated with obesity.

Shape Up America!; 808 17th Street, NW, Suite 600, Washington, DC 20006; (202) 974-5051; *www.shapeup.org*; is a national initiative to promote healthy weight and increased physical activity involving a coalition of industry, medical/health, nutrition, physical fitness, and related organizations. The program is committed to providing science-based health messages so that people will understand the importance of healthy weight and increased physical activity.

Helpful Books

Gastric Bypass Surgery: Everything You Need to Know to Make an Informed Decision (Mary P. McGowan, New York: McGraw-Hill, 2004).

Get with the Program: Getting Real about Your Weight, Health, and Emotional Well-Being (Bob Green, New York: Simon and Schuster, 2002).

Healing Bodies and Souls: A Practical Guide for Congregations (W. Daniel Hale and Harold G. Koenig, Minneapolis: Fortress Press, 2003).

The Thin Commandments Diet: The Ten No-Fail Strategies for Permanent Weight Loss (Stephen Gullo, Emmaus, PA: Rodale Press, 2005).

The Ultimate Weight Solution: The 7 Keys to Weight Loss Freedom (Phil McGraw, New York: Free Press, 2004).

References

Aronne, L. J. (2001). Epidemiology, morbidity, and treatment of overweight and obesity. *Journal of Clinical Psychiatry,* 62 (Suppl. 23), 13–22.

Baldwin, K. A., Humbles, P. L., Armmer, F. A., and Cramer, M. (2001). Perceived health needs of urban African American church congregants. *Public Health Nursing,* 18(5), 295–303.

Bartlett, S. J., Wadden, T. A., and Vogt, R. A. (1996). Psychosocial consequences of weight cycling. *Journal of Consulting and Clinical Psychology,* 64(3), 587–592.

Borrud, L. G., McPherson, R. S., Nichaman, M. Z., Pillow, P. C., and Newell, G. R. (1989). Development of a food frequency instrument:

Ethnic differences in food sources. *Nutrition and Cancer,* 12, 201–211.

Calle, E. E., Rodriguez, C., Walker-Thurmond, K., and Thun, M. J. (2003). Overweight, obesity and mortality from cancer in a prospectively studied cohort of U.S. adults. *New England Journal of Medicine,* 348, 1625–1628.

Cotugna, N., Subar, A. F., Heimendinger, J., and Kahle, L. (1992). Nutrition and cancer prevention knowledge, beliefs, attitudes, and practices: The 1987 National Health Interview Survey. *Journal of the American Dietetic Association,* 8, 963–968.

Davis, N. L., Clance, P. R., and Gailis, A. T. (1999). Treatment approaches for obese and overweight African American women: A consideration of cultural dimensions. *Psychotherapy: Theory, Research, Practice, Training,* 36(1), 27–35.

Dessio, W., Wade, C., Chao, M., Kronenberg, F., Cushman, L. E., and Kalmuss, D. (2004). Religion, spirituality, and healthcare choices of African-American women: Results of a national survey. *Ethnic Diseases,* 14(2), 189–197.

Fobi, M. A. (2004). Surgical treatment of obesity: A review. *Journal of the National Medical Association,* 96(1), 61–75.

Khaodhiar, L., and Blackburn, G. L. (2002). Obesity treatment: Factors involved in weight-loss maintenance and regain. *Current Opinion in Endocrinology and Diabetes,* 9, 369–374.

Klauer, J., and Aronne, L. J. (2002). Managing overweight and obesity in women. *Clinical Obstetrics and Gynecology,* 45(4), 1080–1088.

Kumanyika, S. K., and Charleson, J. B. (1992). Lose weight and win: A church-based weight loss program for blood pressure control among black women. *Patient Education and Counseling,* 19(1), 19–32.

Levin, J., Chatters, L. M., and Taylor, R. J. (2005). Religion, health and medicine in African Americans: Implications for physicians. *Journal of the National Medical Association,* 97(2), 237–249.

National Center for Health Statistics. (2000). Prevalence of overweight and obesity among adults: United States, 1999. Retrieved April 15, 2005, from *www.cdc.gov/nchs/products/pubs/pubd/hestats/obese/obse99.htm.*

Pronk, N. P., and Wing, R. R. (1994). Physical activity and long-term maintenance of weight loss. *Obesity Research,* 2, 587–599.

Sbrocco, T., Carter, M. M., Lewis, E. L., Vaughn, N. A., Kalupa, K. L., King, S., Suchday, S., Osborn, R. L., and Cintron, J. A. (2005). Church-based obesity treatment for African-American women improves adherence. *Ethnic Diseases,* 15(2), 246–255.

Serdula, M. K., Mokdad, A. H., Williamson, D. F., Galuska, D. A., Mendlein, J. M., and Heath, G. W. (1999). Prevalence of attempting weight loss and strategies for controlling weight. *Journal of the American Medical Association,* 282(14), 1353–1358.

Spence-Jones, G. (2003). Overview of obesity. *Critical Care Nursing Quarterly,* 26(2), 83–88.

Troiano, R. P., Flegal, K. M., Kuczmarski, R. J., Campbell, S. M., and Johnson, C. L. (1995). Overweight prevalence and trends for children and adolescents. *Archives of Pediatric Adolescent Medicine,* 149, 1085–1091.

Wadden, T. A., Womble, L. G., Stunkard, A. J., and Anderson, D. A. (2002). Psychosocial consequences of obesity and weight loss. In T. A. Wadden and A. J. Stunkard (Eds.), *Handbook of obesity treatment* (pp. 144–169). New York: Guilford Press.

Yanek, L. R., Becker, D. M., Moy, T. F., Gittelsohn, J., and Koffman, D. M. (2001). Project Joy: Faith based cardiovascular health promotion for African American women. *Public Health Reports,* 116, Suppl. 1, 68–81.

Prescription Drug Dependence/Abuse

"I'm just a bundle of nerves"

Joann is a 67-year-old resident of a retirement community where George, her former pastor, volunteers each week to hold a worship service. Joann is disabled from an automobile accident three years ago that left her crippled and her husband dead. She has struggled emotionally and physically since then.

It is Monday, and Pastor George is leading the weekly worship service for about 15 people. Joann is usually among the most attentive and involved ones in the group. For the past few weeks, though, he has noticed that she has been groggy, her head nodding frequently, and in the last service she nearly went to sleep. Joann nodding off during worship has been routine, especially over the past month. Although Pastor George recognizes that his sermons may not be the most exciting, they hold the interest of the other residents and they used to hold Joann's attention, too. After the service, he walks over and greets her. "Joann, it is good to see you today. How have you been doing?"

Joann responds, "I'm sorry about not being able to stay awake. I think I'm taking too much medication." Pastor George answers, "Don't worry about it, Joann. The important thing is that you come, and I'm always glad to see you here. I am concerned that you think you're taking too much medicine. Why don't I stop by when I'm here Friday and we can discuss this further?" Joanne says, "That would be great. I'll look forward to seeing you about 10:00 a.m."

On Friday morning Pastor George raps on Joann's door. Nobody answers. After about five minutes of knocking, she finally comes to the door. It is about 10:30 in the morning. Joann is still in her nightclothes, and she looks surprised to see Pastor George. After talking briefly at the door, he realizes that she is disoriented and does not recognize him. "Joann, I'm Pastor George. On Monday we talked about my coming over today for a visit." Yawning, she says, "Now I remember. I'm sorry for not being ready. Give me a few minutes to change." Joann makes her way to the bedroom and shuts the door. Pastor George takes a seat. He notices that the apartment looks disheveled. There are clothes lying around, unwashed dishes in the sink, and the room smells of urine.

Joann finally returns and sits down in the living room. Groggily she says, "I'm sorry, but I completely forgot about our visit. I haven't been feeling myself lately. I'm just a bundle of nerves." Pastor George responds, "What's been going on?"

Joann answers, "I haven't been feeling right for a while. Even after all this time, I still can't believe that Tom is gone. And here I am crippled and hardly able to care for myself. My nerves have been shot since the accident, and they seem to be getting worse. I wonder if life is worth all this." Joann covers her face with her hands and begins to cry.

After giving her a chance to sob for a few moments, Pastor George gently inquires, "When did you begin feeling this way?" Joann replies, "It all goes back to that accident. It's so lonely around here without Tom. Sometimes I feel like I'm going crazy."

The pastor responds, "Have you seen a doctor about how you're feeling?" She says, "Yes, but my doctor just gives me another prescription for my nerves. The medicine helps for a while, but I'm having to take it more and more often to help me cope. When I've tried to cut down on the number of pills I take, my nerves get really bad. I don't think I could survive without that medicine."

Pastor George asks, "Can you show me all the medication you're taking?" Joann returns with a handful of bottles. "Here they are," she offers, handing them to him. He carefully reads the labels: one bottle for heart arrhythmias, one for her thyroid, one for diabetes, one to help her sleep at night (temazepam), and one for her nerves (diazepam). He recognizes the diazepam pills (Valium).

"Joann," he asks, "how many of these (pointing to the diazepam) do you take each day?" She answers, "I've been taking those about three or four times a day for the last couple months, but they're not helping as much as they used to." Pastor George continues, "How about this one (pointing to the temazepam)?" Joann states, "Usually only once at night, but sometimes I take two if I'm having a really bad night." Pastor George says, "Joann, I think I'll look up these medications on the Internet to see what their side effects are. The way you feel now may be related to these drugs. I wonder if you're getting the *right* medications for the problems that you are having. I'll call you tonight after doing a little research on this." Before he leaves, Pastor George asks her a final question. "Joann, did you ever have difficulties like this before the accident? Problems with your nerves or anything?" She responds, "Not that I recall. I never went through anything like this until the accident."

That evening, Pastor George looks up the two drugs. He discovers that long-term use of these medications, especially at the doses that Joann is taking, can result in significant side effects — many resembling the problems that she appears to be having.

Pastoral Assessment

Joann is having difficultly staying awake during the day and trouble sleeping at night. Her memory and concentration seem impaired, but are not bad for her age, and she is thinking in a rational manner. She realizes that she needs help and feels overwhelmed by her inability to obtain it. It is possible that Joann may be suffering from untreated depression that could be the root cause for much of her anxiety and "nerves," since depression in later life is often accompanied by anxiety. Her medications show that she has other health problems, too, that might be complicating things.

Pastor George responded appropriately. First, he noticed that Joann did not seem like her usual self during worship services. Second, he checked with her to see if there was a problem. Third, he offered to discuss the situation more thoroughly with Joann when he had a little more time (and also see her in the natural environment of her home). Fourth, he gently explored the problem with her and promised to do further research before making a recommendation.

Relevant History Joann is not behaving like her usual self. During worship, it seems like she is drugged or not getting enough sleep. Joann is receptive to the pastor, so this opens the door for him to pursue the problem. He finds that things are worse than he originally thought — she is groggy, unkempt and not dressed appropriately. Joann is having serious difficulties caring for herself and maintaining the cleanliness of her apartment. She is also having some memory impairment, demonstrated by her forgetting about the pastor's visit.

Joann is having serious emotional problems as well. She admits that her nerves are bad and are not being helped satisfactorily by her medication. She is also feeling depressed and lonely, wondering at times whether life is worth living (an alarming statement). Joann's doctor does not seem to be tuned in to her problems.

Finally, Joann is taking a lot of medication. The doses of diazepam and temazepam that she is taking are much too high for her age. They are likely to build up in her body and interfere with her level of alertness, memory, and balance, while at the same time becoming less effective over time as her body accommodates to their effects. Her doctor has not recognized these problems. The physician is over-prescribing, and Joann is suffering as a result.

Diagnostic Criteria Joann fulfills the criteria for *prescription drug dependence* and may also have an untreated major depressive disorder (American Psychiatric Association, 2000). The criteria for prescription drug dependence include a maladaptive pattern of substance use leading to significant impairment or distress, as indicated by at least three of the following:

1. tolerance, as defined by the need for increased amounts of substance to achieve a desired effect;

2. withdrawal symptoms when the person cannot have access to the substance (or when the effects of the substance wear off before the next scheduled dose);

3. substance taken in larger amounts over a longer period than intended;

4. unsuccessful efforts to cut down or control the use of the substance;

5. a great deal of time spent trying to acquire the substance (such as frequent visits to doctors and/or use of multiple pharmacies);

6. important social or recreational activities reduced or stopped because of use of the substance;

7. substance use continued despite knowledge of ongoing physical or psychological problems that may be caused or made worse by the drug (APA, 2000).

Joann fulfills criteria #1, #2, #3, #4, and #6, which indicate this diagnosis. This applies to her use of diazepam (Valium) in particular.

Prescription drug *dependence* (which Joann has) is different from prescription drug *abuse* and can be distinguished from it. The latter involves a maladaptive pattern of prescription drug use that leads to significant impairment or distress, as indicated by any one of the following during a 12-month period:

1. drug use resulting in failure to fulfill major role obligations either on the job, within the family, or concerning the self (ability to care for basic needs);

2. recurrent use of the drug in situations that the person knows may be physically hazardous;

3. recurrent legal problems due to use of the drug;

4. continued use of the drug despite persistent social or interpersonal problems that are known to be due to use of the substance (American Psychiatric Association, 2000).

None of the above criteria apply to Joann because she is not aware that the drugs she is taking have potentially dangerous side effects or are causing her problems. Her doctor is responsible for that and has allowed this to occur either because of his lack of expertise or simply because of neglect.

Prescription drug dependence is a big problem for seniors. Persons over age 65, while making up only 14 percent of the population, use 25 to 30 percent of all prescription drugs (Ondus et al., 1999). Older adults take an average of eight to ten prescription and non-prescription drugs on a regular basis. Diazepam (Valium) is a particular favorite, despite the fact that it builds up in body fat and stays in the system for a long time, interfering with central nervous system functioning. Large studies have found that Valium is the fifth most commonly prescribed drug, taken by nearly 4 percent of elderly men and 7 percent of elderly women. Between 12 to 18 percent of the U.S. population has used benzodiazepines, the class of drugs to which Valium belongs (Griffiths and Sannerud, 1987). They are primarily used to treat anxiety, insomnia, or panic attacks. In addition to Valium, the most widely used benzodiazepines today are alprazolam (Xanax), clonazepam (Klonopin), and lorazepam (Ativan). Klonopin and Ativan are shorter acting and do not build up in the body as much as Valium and so are safer to use at low doses. Xanax is highly addicting and must be used with caution in the elderly (Mühlberg et al., 1997).

Response to Vignette

Joann is dependent on Valium, and probably to a lesser extent on temazepam, another benzodiazepine. She needs professional help to reduce the doses of these drugs and be placed on a medication that will treat her depression and anxiety, without having the negative side-effects associated with benzodiazepines. This can probably be done as an outpatient, although the treating physician will need to have considerable expertise and skill in working with addictive and emotional disorders in elderly patients.

The pastor's primary task in Joann's situation is to assess, educate, support, and encourage her. He should urge her to obtain a complete medical and psychiatric evaluation from a specialist in these matters. Joann may need much encouragement and support before she will see a physician other than her current doctor, who may have treated her for many years. She will also need psychological support to stop using the drugs. These substances have become familiar to her and provide her with at least some degree of relief (even though the cost of that relief has been getting higher and higher). Finally, she will need support coping with issues related to the death of her husband and her accident-related disability. These latter factors, which have not been fully dealt with, may be causing or worsening her depression/anxiety.

Nevertheless, Joann also has personal resources that need to be fully utilized as her pastor tries to help her. These include Joann's religious faith and relationships with other members of her faith community. This is the time to begin tapping into her spiritual resources, while also being sure that her drugs get straightened out and she is well connected to a medical-psychiatric specialist. Religious faith has been shown to predict faster recovery from depression and anxiety and can provide her the strength to get off the drugs. Among the most effective programs for helping persons with alcohol or drugs (whether prescribed, over-the-counter, legal, or illegal) is Alcoholics or Narcotics Anonymous (AA or NA). The treatment provided by these organizations is grounded on three spiritual principles:

1. admitting that one has lost control over an addiction and is unable to overcome the problem without help;

2. relying on a Higher Power to provide strength to resist falling back into addiction; and

3. making a commitment to others in a community and becoming accountable for one's actions to them.

Every one of these principles should be active within Joann's faith community.

Treatment within the Faith Community

If the pastor can rally her church around Joann, it can provide much of the help that organizations such as AA or NA do. However, the advantage of groups like AA or NA is that they connect people with others who have struggled with and overcome the same problems that they have (as opposed to members of the faith community, most of whom will have no personal experience with dependence or addiction). In any case, whatever the pastor can do to help support and nourish Joann's religious faith will likely increase her success at getting off of benzodiazepines and coping with the loss of her husband and her accident-related disability.

In general, the faith community can play a significant role, as Pastor George did, in helping to identify individuals in the congregation who are showing signs of stress or other mental or physical health problems and in getting them to trained professionals for help. Members of the faith community can provide emotional support to persons during their rehabilitation and help reintegrate them into the social life of the church. Specifically, members can volunteer to help by visiting or calling, providing rides or accompanying them to the doctor's office, or simply offering a listening ear on a regular basis.

Indications for Referral

Anyone who meets the criteria for prescription drug dependence or abuse needs immediate referral for professional care. In Joann's case, she needs both expert medical referral (for the physical problems that may be contributing to her symptoms) and expert psychiatric referral (for drug tapering and appropriate treatment of her depression). Members of the faith community should keep in mind that older adults may take benzodiazepines or other sedatives for a legitimate reason and not jump to the conclusion that there is a problem — when actually there is not. It is also essential that any interventions, no matter how benign, be carried out with the explicit consent of the person being helped. Only in an emergency, where someone's life is in danger or physical injury is imminent, should the need for a person's consent be overruled in favor of ensuring their safety.

Joann needs to be evaluated by someone other than her current physician. He has already proven that he lacks the interest and expertise to handle her case appropriately. Therefore, she should be referred to either a geriatric medicine specialist (to ensure her medical problems are stable) and/or a geriatric psychiatrist (to manage her addiction and any other emotional issues). Joann needs a comprehensive physical and psychological evaluation. Then she will require a carefully managed rehabilitation plan as she is tapered off benzodiazepines, started on antidepressant medication, and connected to a therapist who can help her develop effective coping strategies for her loneliness, anxiety, and depression. Non-drug treatments to help control her anxiety, such as biofeedback or cognitive-behavioral therapy, may be helpful in addition to drug treatment for her depression.

Treatment by Mental Health Specialist

Evaluation by a geriatric medicine specialist (geriatrician) can be obtained either locally (some medical internists and family physicians have special certification in geriatric medicine) or at a major medical center (typically found in large urban areas). The same applies to obtaining an evaluation by a geriatric psychiatrist.

To locate a geriatrician online, a commercial organization called "HealthGrades" offers physician locator services, which will provide a list of up to 20 geriatricians in a local area. See *http://healthgrades.com/consumer/index.cfm?*. A geriatric psychiatrist can be identified in your local area by going to the American Association for Geriatric Psychiatry's website: *www.aagponline.org/about/referrals.asp*. A geriatric psychiatrist can be identified in your local area (free) by going to the American

Association for Geriatric Psychiatry's website: *www.aagponline.org/about/referrals.asp*.

Cross-Cultural Issues The cultural background of persons may influence how willing they are to tolerate unpleasant physical symptoms (pain) or emotional symptoms (anxiety). Drug dependence tends to be less common in societies where pain and suffering are accepted as a normal part of life. People from affluent societies tend not to be willing to tolerate unpleasant symptoms, and they may be inclined to seek quick relief that ultimately leads to drug abuse or dependence.

Resources Information on all drugs prescribed by physicians can be obtained by consulting a recent copy of the Physicians' Desk Reference (PDR). Local libraries may have the most recent PDR edition. Most online pharmacies allow a person to "search" the name of common prescription medications and provide information about side effects. Online pharmacy websites include:

> *www.rxlist.com*
> *www.healthsquare.com/drugmain.htm*
> *medi-smart.com/pharm.html*

American Academy of Addiction Psychiatry; 1010 Vermont Avenue, NW, Suite 710, Washington, DC 20005; (202) 393-4484; *www.aaap.org*.

American Academy for Geriatric Psychiatry; 7910 Woodmont Avenue, Suite 1050, Bethesda, MD 20814; (301) 654-7850; *www.aagponline.org*.

American Psychiatric Association; 1000 Wilson Boulevard, Suite 1825, Arlington, VA 22209; (703) 907-7300; *www.psych.org*.

American Psychological Association; 750 First Street, NE, Washington, DC 20002; (800) 374-2721; *www.apa.org*.

American Society of Addiction Medicine; 4601 North Park Avenue, Upper Arcade #101, Chevy Chase, MD 20815; (301) 656-3920;

www.asam.org; is a medical society dedicated to educating physicians and improving the treatment of individuals suffering from addictions.

National Institute on Drug Abuse; National Institutes of Health, 6001 Executive Boulevard, Rockville, MD 20852; (301) 443-1124; *www.drugabuse.gov.*

SMART Recovery (Self-Management And Recovery Training); 7537 Mentor Avenue, Suite 306, Mentor, OH 44060; (866) 951-5357; *www.smartrecovery.org*; is a national network of self-help groups for individuals wanting to gain their independence from addictive and compulsive behaviors. It is an abstinence program based on cognitive-behavioral principles, especially those of rational-emotive-behavior therapy. It provides information and referrals, literature and assistance in starting local chapters.

Helpful Books

Addiction by Prescription (Joan E. Gadsby, Toronto: Key Porter Books, 2001).

Prescription Drug Abuse and Dependence: How Prescription Drug Abuse Contributes to the Drug Abuse Epidemic (Daniel P. Greenfield, Springfield, IL: Charles C. Thomas, 1994).

Prescription Drug Addiction: The Hidden Epidemic (Rod Colvin, Omaha, NE: Addicus Books, 2002).

References

American Psychiatric Association. (2000). *Diagnostic and statistical manual of mental disorders* (4th edition, text revision). Washington, DC: American Psychiatric Association.

Griffiths, R., and Sannerud, C. (1987). Abuse of and dependence on benzodiazepines and other anxiolytic/sedative drugs. In H. Meltzer (Ed.), *Psychopharmacology: The third generation of progress*. New York: Raven Press, pp. 1535–1541.

Mühlberg, W., Rieck, W., Arnold, E., Ott, G., and Lungershausen, E. (1997). Pharmacokinetics of alprazolam in elderly patients with multiple diseases. *Archives of Gerontology and Geriatrics*, 25(1), 91–100.

Ondus, K. A., Hujer, M. E., Mann, A. E., and Mion, L. C. (1999). Substance abuse and the hospitalized elderly. *Orthopedic Nursing*, 18(4), 27–36.

Steroids

"He had been tempted to start taking pills"

Seventeen-year-old Chris, an active church member, asked to meet with his pastor, Rev. Paul Edgar. Chris is a promising high school basketball player who has been scouted by several nationally recognized colleges. While no one questions Chris's talent, there is a problem. At 6'4" and 160 pounds, he is on the lean side for college basketball. Chris came to confess to his pastor that over the last several weeks he had been tempted to start taking anabolic steroids to bulk up and develop the muscle mass he felt he needed. Several athletes at school were taking them, and Chris wanted the advice of his pastor, who had been a star hockey player in his youth. Rev. Edgar confessed that he knew little about steroids but what he had heard was not good. The pastor promised to research the subject and made an appointment to talk with Chris in a few days.

Rev. Edgar found that anabolic steroids are synthetic derivatives of the male hormone testosterone. Like testosterone, steroids cause the muscles to grow. "Anabolic" refers to the building of skeletal muscle, and "steroids" are the category of drugs. In general, the drugs build muscle tissue and allow muscles to recover more quickly after being used. They do nothing to improve endurance, help performance, or enhance a player's skill (Lenehan, 2003).

Pastoral Assessment

These drugs are available legally only by prescription from a licensed physician, who must closely supervise their use. It is illegal for individuals to sell steroids. They are sometimes prescribed to treat patients with AIDS or other diseases that cause the loss of large amounts of lean muscle mass (Creutzberg and Schols, 1999). Most steroids that are used without a prescription are smuggled in from other countries, diverted from U.S. pharmacies illegally, or synthesized in clandestine laboratories. More than 100 different anabolic steroids have been developed. Their common street (slang) names include: arnolds, gym candy, pumpers, roids, stackers, weight trainers, and juice (Lenehan, 2003).

Abuse of anabolic steroids can lead to serious, sometimes irreversible, health problems. They can halt bone growth and damage the heart, kidneys, and liver (Kuipers, 1998). Young people who take anabolic steroids without having a medical need for them are playing Russian roulette with their bodies. Rev. Edgar advised Chris that taking steroids was dangerous to his health and against the law and there were other things he could do to increase his strength.

Relevant History   One of the main reasons individuals abuse steroids is to try to improve their performance in sports. Athletes take them in the hope of gaining weight, strength, power, speed, endurance, and aggressiveness. They are widely used by those involved in track and field (mostly the throwing events), weightlifting, and football. Results from a 2003 national survey of students in eighth, tenth, and twelfth grades showed that 2.5 percent of eighth graders, 3 percent of tenth graders, and 3.5 percent of twelfth graders reported using steroids at least once in their lifetime (U.S. Department of Health and Human Services, 2004). This same study found that 21.7 percent of eighth graders, 30.6 percent of tenth graders, and 40.7 percent of twelfth graders stated that steroids were "fairly easy" or "very easy" to obtain. Fifty-five percent of twelfth graders reported that using steroids was a "great risk" (U.S. Department of Health and Human Services, 2004).

When a person takes steroids, the normal balance of hormones is disrupted. Hormonal confusion can lead to female bodily traits in men, and women can take on male traits (Fahey, 1998). Men, for example, can grow breasts and women can grow facial and excessive body hair and develop deep voices. Both sexes can experience male-pattern baldness. Many users develop severe acne.

Anabolic steroids are particularly dangerous for adolescents because their bones are still developing. When there is an excess of hormones, the brain is fooled into thinking that the body has already gone through puberty, so it signals the bones to stop growing. That means teens may never reach their full stature. In addition, steroids can harm the heart, causing potentially fatal heart attacks, and seriously damage the liver (Kuipers, 1998).

Anabolic steroids cause problems in the brain as well. Because of their effect on the limbic system, a part of the brain connected with mood, some users experience uncontrolled outbursts of anger, frustration, or combativeness (Porcerelli and Sandler, 1998). This condition is known as "roid rage" (short for "steroid rage"). Besides "roid rage," steroid users may experience mood swings, forgetfulness, and difficulty sleeping. Most steroid users take pills, but some inject the drugs. Needle sharing can lead to the spread of hepatitis, HIV, and AIDS.

Doses taken by abusers can be up to 100 times greater than amounts used to treat medical conditions. Anabolic steroids often are taken in combination in a practice called "stacking," in which the abuser mixes oral and/or injectable types of anabolic steroids (Lenehan, 2003). Some steroid abusers also employ a practice called "pyramiding," where they gradually increase doses then slowly decrease them to nil. The belief that these methods produce bigger muscles has no scientific support.

An undetermined number of steroid abusers become addicted to the drugs, as evidenced by their continuing to take steroids in spite of physical problems and negative effects on social relations. In addition, abusers spend large amounts of time and money obtaining the drugs, as well as experiencing withdrawal symptoms, including mood swings, fatigue, restlessness, loss of appetite, insomnia, reduced sex drive, depression, and the desire to take more steroids (Gruber and Pope, 2000).

Response to Vignette

After researching the relationship between sports and steroids, Rev. Edgar realized that it was important for Chris to understand that he can excel in basketball and gain added strength without drugs. Chris needs to focus his energy and time on eating a healthy diet, getting proper rest, and maintaining good overall mental and physical health. The parish nurse was knowledgeable about nutrition and was able to give Chris ongoing guidance about a nutritious diet that could help him gain bulk and strength. There was also a group of middle-aged body-builders in the church who took him under their wing and helped him maintain and improve his strength through weightlifting. These activities not only improved his conditioning but also forged new bonds of fellowship for him in the church.

Treatment within the Faith Community

The knowledge that Rev. Edgar, the parish nurse, and Chris obtained about steroids motivated them to organize an educational seminar for the church youth group. Their goal was to alert teens to the harmful effects of anabolic steroids and the positive alternatives provided by nutrition and conditioning. The program was based upon current research in the field showing that such information can increase healthy behaviors and reduce steroid use among high school athletes (MacKinnon et al., 2001). The presenters encouraged the church youth to share this new information with friends and teammates and to take a stand against the use of steroids and other drugs. They were invited to speak to several other youth groups in the community during the next year, and an area-wide Christian weight-lifting group was formed as a result of their work.

Indications for Referral

Rev. Edgar was able to give Chris the sort of counseling and guidance he needed. However, it is important that clergy understand the limits of their training and know when to ask for help from specialists. Youngsters using anabolic steroids will often benefit from a referral to a mental health professional who can evaluate and treat underlying issues that may be the reason for the abuse. A physician can help determine whether there are medical problems related to the steroid use.

Treatment by Mental Health Specialist

For long-term steroid abusers who become addicted, the most dangerous of the withdrawal symptoms is depression, because it sometimes leads to suicide attempts. Untreated, some depressive symptoms associated with anabolic steroid withdrawal have been known to persist for a year or more after a person stops taking the drugs (Gruber and Pope, 2000).

Treatment for depression is one of the genuine success stories in mental health. A combination of medication and cognitive-behavioral therapy is the standard and frequently successful treatment for most depression. There are several groups of non-addictive medications available to treat depression, and they can affect individuals differently (Preston et al., 2001). Their beneficial effects are achieved by restoring the levels of brain chemicals that are depleted when an individual is depressed. It is important for patients to work with their physicians to find the most beneficial choice.

Cross-Cultural Issues

Anabolic steroid abuse is an international problem. For example, a Swedish study examined the incidence of the misuse of anabolic steroids among adolescents in Sweden. An anonymous questionnaire was completed by 5,827 male and female pupils aged 16 and 17. Among 16-year-old males, 3.6 percent had misused anabolic steroids, while 2.8 percent of the older group said they had. These boys had also abused alcohol, growth hormones, and narcotic drugs more than non-users of steroid hormones. There was no reported use of steroids among girls in the study. The findings support the need for preventive work among Swedish male adolescents to reduce the misuse of anabolic steroids (Nilsson et al., 2001).

In a separate study, researchers interviewed 100 Australian anabolic steroid users. The median age of the group was 27 years and 94 percent were male. More than three of four users (78 percent) had at least one symptom of steroid abuse or dependence. A total of 23 percent of the participants were diagnosed as dependent and a further 25 percent met criteria for abuse (Copeland et al., 2000).

Resources American Academy of Addiction Psychiatry; 1010 Vermont Avenue, NW, Suite 710, Washington, DC 20005; (202) 393-4484; *www.aaap .org.*

American Academy of Child and Adolescent Psychiatry has a website with free information on teen problems, including drug abuse, at *www.aacap.org.*

American Council for Drug Education; 164 West 74th Street, New York, NY 10023; (800) 883-DRUG; *www.acde.org.*

American Society of Addiction Medicine; 4601 North Park Avenue, Upper Arcade, Suite 101, Chevy Chase, MD 20815; (301) 656-3920; *www.asam.org;* is a medical society dedicated to educating physicians and improving the treatment of individuals suffering from alcoholism and other addictions.

Fellowship of Christian Athletes; 8709 Leeds Road, Kansas City, MO 64129; (816) 921-0909; *www.fca.org.* The Fellowship's "One Way to Play" offers young people a comprehensive program aimed at positive opportunities and drug-free lifestyles.

Join Together; 441 Stuart Street, Boston, MA 02166; (617) 437-1500; *www.jointogether.org*; a national resource center for communities working to reduce substance abuse and gun violence.

National Center on Addiction and Substance Abuse at Columbia University; 152 West 57th Street, 12th floor, New York, NY 10019; (212) 841-5200; *www.casacolumbia.org.*

National Clearinghouse for Alcohol and Drug Information; P.O. Box 2345, Rockville, MD 20847; (800) 729-6686; *www.health.org*;

provides free, useful materials about the many aspects of adolescent alcohol and drug abuse, treatment, and prevention. Several of these publications are designed for the faith community.

National Federation of State High School Associations; 11724 NW Plaza Circle, Kansas City, MO 64153; (816) 464-5400 ext. 3263; *www.nfhs.org*; serves over 10 million youth who participate in school activities. Their Drugs and Sports Course provides coaches with training in preventing substance abuse.

National High School Athletic Coaches Association; P.O. Box 2569, Gig Harbor, WA 98335; (253) 853-6777; *www.hscoaches.org*; offers training seminars for coaches in drug prevention and counseling.

National Institute on Drug Abuse, National Institutes of Health; 6001 Executive Boulevard, Room 5213, Bethesda, MD 20892-9561; (301) 443-1124; *www.drugabuse.gov.*

Safe and Drug-Free Schools, Office of Elementary and Secondary Education, U.S. Department of Education; 600 Independence Avenue, SW, Washington, DC 20202-0498; (800) 624-0100; *www.ed.gov/offices/OESE*; the federal government's principal program for reducing drug use and violence through education and prevention activities in our nation's schools.

Anabolic Steroids: And Other Performance Enhancing Drugs (Pat Lenehan, New York: Taylor and Francis, 2003). **Helpful Books**

Anabolic Steroids and the Athlete (William N. Taylor, Jefferson, NC: McFarland and Company, 2002).

Anabolic Steroids in Sport and Exercise (Charles Yesalis, Champaign, IL: Human Kinetics Publishers, 2000).

Anabolics 2004 (William Llewellyn, Boise, ID: Molecular Nutrition, 2003).

Diets Designed for Athletes: How to Combine Foods, Fluids, and Supplements for Maximum Training and Performance (Maryann Karinch, Champaign, IL: Human Kinetics Publishers, 2001).

Steroids, Sports, and Body Image: The Risks of Performance-Enhancing Drugs (Judy Monroe, Berkeley Heights, NJ: Enslow Publishers, 2004). Ages 12 and up.

References   Copeland, J., Peters, R., and Dillon, P. (2000). Anabolic-androgenic steroid use disorders among a sample of Australian competitive and recreational users. *Drug and Alcohol Dependence, 60*(1), 91–96.

Creutzberg, E. C., and Schols, A. M. (1999). Anabolic steroids. *Current Opinion Clinical Nutrition and Metabolic Care, 2*(3), 243–253.

Fahey, T. D. (1998). Anabolic-androgenic steroids: Mechanism of action and effects on performance. In *Encyclopedia of sports medicine and science,* T. D. Fahey (Ed.). *Internet Society for Sport Science.* Retrieved March 7, 1998, from *www.sportsci.org.*

Gruber, A. J., and Pope, H. G. (2000). Psychiatric and medical effects of anabolic-androgenic steroid use in women. *Psychotherapy and Psychosomatics, 69,* 19–26.

Kuipers, H. (1998). Anabolic steroids: Side effects. In *Encyclopedia of sports medicine and science,* T. D. Fahey (Ed.). *Internet Society for Sport Science.* Retrieved March 7, 1998, from *www.sportsci.org.*

Lenehan, P. (2003). *Anabolic steroids: And other performance enhancing drugs.* New York: Taylor and Francis.

MacKinnon, D. P., Goldberg, L., Clarke, G. N., Elliot, D. L., Cheong, J., Lapin, A., Moe, E. L., and Krull, J. L. (2001). Mediating mechanisms in a program to reduce intentions to use anabolic steroids and improve exercise self-efficacy and dietary behavior. *Prevention Science, 2*(1), 15–28.

Nilsson, S., Baigi, A., Marklund, B., and Fridlund, B. (2001). The prevalence of the use of androgenic anabolic steroids by adolescents in a county of Sweden. *European Journal of Public Health, 11*(2), 195–197.

Porcerelli, J. H., and Sandler, B. A. (1998). Anabolic-androgenic steroid abuse and psychopathology. *Psychiatric Clinics of North America, 21*(4), 829–833.

Preston, J. D., O'Neal, J. H., and Talaga, M. (2001). *Handbook of clinical psychopharmacology for therapists*. Oakland, CA: New Harbinger.

U.S. Department of Health and Human Services. (2004). *Monitoring the Future Study*. Rockville, MD: National Institute on Drug Abuse.

Tobacco

"It was the 'cool' thing to do in my group"

Helen began smoking at 14 years of age. She would secretly have a few cigarettes with her friends in the evenings when they were away from their homes. Helen was able to buy cigarettes almost anyplace they were sold. Her parents would have been furious with her if they had found out, though they were both smokers themselves. They did not learn that she smoked until Helen was 16 years old. By then she was hooked. That was 20 years ago.

She went to see her pastor, Rev. Janice Turner, to talk about her struggle with smoking and to seek advice about how she might quit. Helen said, "I never thought of the damage I was doing to myself when I was young. Smoking was exciting, and I felt like a grown-up, even though I had a bad cough after a cold and my teeth weren't as white as the teeth of the girls who didn't smoke. Most of my friends smoked, so it was the 'cool' thing to do in our group."

She met and married her husband, Alan, another heavy smoker, when they were 20. She had three children and life was relatively normal. She explained, "We smoked around our children, never thinking it was doing them any harm. They begged us to stop when they learned about the dangers of smoking, but we brushed off their pleas. We weren't going to die — that happened to other people!" Now her father, aged 59, has lung cancer. This has motivated Helen to try to stop smoking, but she is afraid she does not have the strength to succeed.

**Pastoral
Assessment** Tobacco use is the chief preventable cause of premature disease and death in the United States. Despite the well-publicized dangers of smoking, some 46.5 million American adults currently smoke cigarettes (Centers for Disease Control and Prevention, 2002). Nearly one of every five deaths is due to tobacco use (McGinnis and Foege, 1993), and the annual health care expenditure for treating smoking-related illnesses was estimated in 1993 at $274 for every adult American (Miller et al., 1999). Each year more than 400,000 Americans die from smoking-related illnesses and 2 million die in all developing countries combined (Peto et al., 1994). Smoking kills more Americans annually than AIDS, automobile accidents, suicides, murders, fires, alcohol, and illegal drugs combined (CDC, 1994).

The early adolescent years (ages 11 through 15) are the crucial life stage for preventing smoking, and it is rare for tobacco use to begin after high school (Johnston et al., 1995). Each day nearly 3,000 American youth begin smoking (An et al., 1999). Rates of tobacco use among teenagers in the United States increased from 27.5 percent in 1991 to 36.4 percent in 1997 (*Morbidity and Mortality Weekly,* 1998) with a similar trend seen in Canada (Spurgeon, 1999). It is estimated that between one-third and one-half of adolescents who try only a few cigarettes will become regular smokers, a process that takes an average of two to three years (Henningfield et al., 1991).

In the United States, annual illegal sales of tobacco to minors total 950 million packs of cigarettes and 26 million containers of smokeless tobacco (Heishman et al., 1997). About one-half of minors who attempt to purchase tobacco products in stores report never being asked for proof of age (CDC, 1996). Minors have even easier access to cigarettes via the Internet because many online vendors have weak or nonexistent age verification procedures. In a recent study, minors successfully received cigarettes 93.6 percent of the time when they attempted to purchase them with a credit card (Ribisl et al., 2003). Internet vendors sent 1,650 packs of cigarettes to the underage adolescents in this study without verifying age for any of the deliveries.

Tobacco is associated with the increased likelihood of using other addictive substances, acting for some as a "gateway drug" (Elders et al., 1994). It is generally the first substance used by teens who later use alcohol and illicit drugs. The surgeon general found that 12-to-17-year-olds who said they had smoked in the past 30 days were three times more likely to have used alcohol, eight times more likely to have smoked marijuana, and 22 times more likely to have used cocaine within the previous 30 days than those teens who had not smoked (Elders et al., 1994).

Relevant History

Nicotine is the drug in tobacco that causes addiction. It is absorbed and enters the bloodstream through the lungs when smoke is inhaled. It is a psychoactive substance with stimulant effects on the activity of the brain. It also has calming properties, especially in times of stress. Although its effects are less dramatic than those of some other addictive substances, nicotine causes activation of "pleasure centers" in the brain, which may explain the enjoyment and addictiveness of smoking.

Diagnostic Criteria

Nicotine dependence is a pattern of compulsive use of nicotine-containing products (cigarettes, chewing tobacco, snuff, pipes, and/or cigars) that results in nicotine tolerance and withdrawal (American Psychiatric Association, 2000). As a person attempts to quit smoking or reduce the amount of nicotine used, several signs of withdrawal can begin within 24 hours, including a depressed mood, insomnia, irritability, frustration, anger, problems with concentration, anxiety, restlessness, and weight gain (APA, 2000). Cigarette smoking has the most intense habit-creating pattern among tobacco products and is the most difficult to quit. There is usually a "craving" (a strong subjective drive) to use cigarettes (APA, 2000). Many individuals who become nicotine-dependent continue to smoke, despite knowledge that they have a medical condition adversely affected by smoking (such as bronchitis).

Smoking rates remain high because once an individual smokes regularly, it is unlikely that he or she will be able to quit easily. In 2000,

15.7 million adult smokers tried to quit smoking, but only 4.7 percent of smokers who reported daily smoking during the previous year were abstinent for 3–12 months that year (CDC, 2002). On average, adolescent boys who start smoking will continue for about 16 years and adolescent girls who start smoking will continue for at least 20 years before being able to quit (Pierce and Gilpin, 1996).

Response to Vignette
Rev. Turner told Helen that being addicted to nicotine does not mean that a person cannot stop — only that it can be difficult to do so. The pastor assured Helen that she would help her find the resources she needed to give her the best chance to quit and that she would continue to support her efforts to stop. Rev. Turner was also able to help Helen talk about some of the grief she was feeling about her dad having lung cancer.

The pastor was able to assist Helen in finding a Nicotine Anonymous group. There is evidence that people who try to stop smoking are more likely to be successful if they have group support than are those who try to quit alone (Garvey et al., 1992). Rev. Turner also made sure that Helen found a psychologist who had experience in working with addictions. The smoking cessation treatment the therapist recommended included a combination of psychological and pharmacological approaches.

Treatment within the Faith Community
Greater religious involvement has been associated with lower risk of use of tobacco and other addictive substances in 26 separate studies conducted in the United States, Great Britain, Nigeria, Australia, Norway, Switzerland, Israel, Canada, France, Scotland, and Ireland (Koenig et al., 2001). Blyth and Leffert (1995) cite a number of studies specifically on teen drug use (including nicotine) that report an inverse relationship between drug use and religious involvement among teens and young adults. Brown and colleagues (2001) examined a nationally representative sample of 188,000 high school classes that graduated

between 1976 and 1997. The investigators found a highly consistent association between lower cigarette use and greater religious involvement across the 22-year period.

A national survey of 2,478 teens found that religious high school seniors were less likely to smoke, and those who did smoke started smoking later than their less religious counterparts. Weekly religious service attenders, teens who said faith was very important, and those who had been involved in a religious youth group for six or more years, were significantly more likely to delay their first use of cigarettes when compared to non-attenders, teens for whom faith was not important, and those who had never been in a religious youth group. While about two in ten of all the teens smoked regularly, three in ten teens who were not involved in religious activities did so. Catholic, Mormon, Jewish, Baptist, and other Protestant students were all less likely to smoke than non-religious students. The inverse relationship between smoking and various measures of religiousness were statistically significant after controlling for race, age, sex, rural/urban residence, region, education of parents, number of siblings, whether the mother is employed, and the presence of a father/male guardian in the household (Smith and Faris, 2002).

If involvement in faith communities has a positive effect on the attitudes and behavior of teens toward smoking cigarettes, then encouraging young people to be engaged in religious life may be beneficial to those seeking to avoid tobacco. Adolescents who join a religious youth group may find it a helpful place to experience peer support that can help them quit smoking. Tobacco use prevention programs for teens would be a valuable ministry of a congregation, especially since survey findings indicate that one in ten teenagers who regularly attend church does smoke (Smith and Faris, 2002). Faith-based intervention programs need to address adolescents' abilities to recognize social and advertising pressures to use tobacco as well as developing skills to resist them (Bruvold, 1993). Increased self-reliance and self-esteem with decreased social alienation appear to be important factors in resisting the pressure to smoke (Bruvold, 1993). Faith-based tobacco-cessation programs focused on minority groups that have high levels of religious participation and suffer a disproportionately higher burden of tobacco-attributable illnesses and deaths may be of particular value (Spangler et al., 1998).

Indications for Referral A referral to a specialist is especially needed for persons with a history of heavy smoking for a long time. Heavy smokers tend to light up soon after waking, during illness, and more often in the morning than the afternoon (American Psychiatric Association, 2000). Individuals who have made repeated attempts to quit smoking without success also require professionally designed smoking-cessation programs.

Treatment by Mental Health Specialist The state-of-the-art smoking-cessation treatments use a combination of psychological and pharmacological approaches (Cepeda-Benito et al., 2004). The psychological interventions often include self-management techniques — setting a time to quit smoking, making plans for coping with the temptation to smoke, and seeking support during periods of high relapse potential.

The most successful pharmacological interventions use a nicotine replacement therapy, either in the form of gum or "the patch," designed to deliver nicotine into the body via the skin. The basic idea behind these is to slowly taper the smoker off of the nicotine in cigarettes by replacing it in a controlled manner, reducing the withdrawal symptoms. Once ex-smokers have stabilized at the level of nicotine replacement, they can begin to bring their intake down in a controlled way (Cepeda-Benito et al., 2004).

Cross-Cultural Issues A British study (Hope and Cook, 2001) examined what the authors called Christian commitment by asking participants if they regularly attended church, prayed, and read the Bible. A fourth question asked if they agreed or disagreed with the statement, "I have given my life to Jesus." All four items made significant contributions to a model predicting lifetime tobacco use (i.e., never smoked) among 12–16-

year-olds from England, Scotland, and Wales. The study, which also examined participants between 17 and 30 years of age, found that the only items that significantly predicted smoking in this age group were Bible reading and giving one's life to Jesus. To Hope and Cook (2001, p. 109), "The findings suggest that for church affiliated young people it is initially the socialization of religion that acts as prohibitory against substance use, though, as age increases, a greater internalization of Christian commitment becomes more important." The primary effect of religion on smoking may be its capacity to inhibit adolescents from trying cigarettes.

Resources

Action on Smoking and Health; 2013 H Street, NW, Washington, DC 20006; (202) 659-4310; *ash.org*; has many resources, including a teen page, on its website.

American Cancer Society; P.O. Box 22718, Oklahoma City, OK 73123-1718; (800) ACS-2345; *www.cancer.org*; annually sponsors the Great American Smokeout.

American Lung Association; 61 Broadway, 6th Floor, New York, NY 10006; (800) 548-8252; *www.lungusa.org*; provides information on the health effects of tobacco use and the latest information on efforts to combat tobacco use among teens.

Campaign for Tobacco-Free Kids; 1400 Eye Street, NW, Suite 1200, Washington, DC 20005; (202) 296-5469; *www.tobaccofreekids.org*.

Corporate Accountability International's Tobacco Industry Campaign; 46 Plympton Street, Boston, MA 02118; (800) 688-8797; *www .stopcorporateabuse.org*; organized to stop the tobacco industry from addicting new customers, especially children and young people.

Foundation for a Smokefree America; P.O. Box 492028, Los Angeles, CA 90049; (310) 471-4270; *www.tobaccofree.com*; founded by R. J. Reynolds's grandson after he saw his father, brother, and other relatives die from cigarette-induced emphysema and cancer.

Nicotine Anonymous World Services; 419 Main Street, PMB #370, Huntington Beach, San Francisco, CA 92648; (415) 750-0328;

www.nicotine-anonymous.org; is an international group with 500 affiliates, founded in 1985. Based on a 12-step model for people who want to recover from nicotine addiction in all forms, it has a newsletter and provides assistance in starting new groups.

NicNet: The Nicotine and Tobacco Network, *www.nicnet.org*, is a large resource for smoking and tobacco Internet links.

Quitnet, *www.quitnet.com*, is an Internet site maintained in association with Boston University School of Public Health. It has useful information for those seeking to stop smoking or those wanting to help others quit.

Helpful Books

American Lung Association: 7 Steps to a Smoke-Free Life (Edwin B. Fisher and Toni L. Goldfarb, New York: Interscience, 1998).

Developing School-Based Tobacco Use Prevention and Cessation Programs (Steve Sussman, Clyde W. Dent, Dee Burton, and Alan W. Stacy, New Berry, CA: Sage Publications, 1995) offers a full picture of the key issues in designing and implementing a school-based prevention and cessation program. Many aspects of this program would be useful in congregational settings.

Dying to Quit: Why We Smoke and How We Stop (Janet Brigham, Washington, DC: Joseph Henry Press, 1998).

Growing Up Tobacco Free: Preventing Nicotine Addiction in Children and Youth (Barbara S. Lynch and Richard J. Bonnie, New York: National Academy Press, 1994). This book addresses prevention programs for youth, explains nicotine's effects, describes the process of addiction, and provides guidelines for public action.

Quit and Stay Quit: A Personal Program to Stop Smoking (Terry A. Rustin, Center City, MN: Hazelden Publishing and Educational Services, 1995).

Quit for Teens: Read This Book and Stop Smoking (Charles F. Wetherall, New York: Andrews and McMeel, 1995) gives reasons for teens to stop smoking, explains why teens smoke, and offers techniques to stop.

Teens and Tobacco: A Fatal Attraction (Susan S. Lang and Beth H. Marks, New York: Twenty-First Century Press, 1996) discusses the effects of smoking on teens and why they smoke.

References

American Psychiatric Association. (2000). *Diagnostic and statistical manual of mental disorders* (4th edition, text revision). Washington, DC: American Psychiatric Association.

An, L. C., O'Malley, P. M., Schulenberg, J., Bachman, J. G., and Johnston, L. D. (1999). Changes at the high end of risk in cigarette smoking among US high school seniors. *American Journal of Public Health,* 89(5), 699–705.

Blyth, D. A., and Leffert, N. (1995). Communities as contexts for adolescent development: An empirical analysis. *Journal of Adolescent Research,* 10(1), 64–87.

Brown, T. N., Schulenberg, J., Backman, J. G., O'Malley, P. M., and Johnston, L. D. (2001). Are risk and protective factors for substance use consistent across historical time? National data from the high school classes of 1976 through 1997. *Prevention Science,* 2(1), 29–43.

Bruvold, W. H. (1993). A meta-analysis of adolescent smoking prevention programs. *American Journal of Public Health,* 83(6), 872–880.

Centers for Disease Control and Prevention. (1994). Cigarette smoking among adults — United States, 1993. *Morbidity and Mortality Weekly Report,* 43, 925–930.

Centers for Disease Control and Prevention. (1996). Tobacco use and usual source of cigarettes among high school students — United States, 1995. *Morbidity and Mortality Weekly Report,* 45, 413–418.

Centers for Disease Control and Prevention. (2002). Cigarette smoking among adults — United States, 2000. *Morbidity and Mortality Weekly Report,* 51, 642–645.

Cepeda-Benito, A., Reynoso, J. T., and Erath, S. (2004). Meta-analysis of the efficacy of nicotine replacement therapy for smoking cessation: Differences between men and women. *Journal of Consulting and Clinical Psychology,* 72(4), 712–722.

Elders, M. J., Perry, C. L., Eriksen, M. P., and Giovino, G. A. (1994). The report of the surgeon general: Preventing tobacco use among young people. *American Journal of Public Health,* 84(4), 543–547.

Garvey, A., Bliss, R., Hitchcock, J., Heinold, J., and Rosner, B. (1992). Predictors of smoking relapse among self-quitters: A report from the normative aging study. *Addictive Behaviors,* 17, 367–377.

Heishman, S. J., Kozlowski, L. T., and Henningfield, J. E. (1997). Nicotine addiction: Implications for public health policy. *Journal of Social Issues,* 53(1), 13–33.

Henningfield, J. E., Cohen, C., and Slade, J. D. (1991). Is nicotine more addictive than cocaine? *British Journal of Addiction,* 86, 565–569.

Hope, L. C., and Cook, C. C. H. (2001). The role of Christian commitment in predicting drug use amongst church affiliated young people. *Mental Health, Religion and Culture,* 4(2), 109–117.

Johnston, L. D., O'Malley, P. M., and Bachman, J. G. (1995). *National survey results on drug use from the Monitoring the Future study, 1975–1994* (NIH Publication No. 95-4026). Washington, DC: U.S. Government Printing Office.

Koenig, H. G., McCullough, M. E., and Larson, D. B. (2001). *Handbook on religion and health.* Oxford: Oxford University Press.

McGinnis, J. M., and Foege, W. H. (1993). Actual causes of death in the United States. *Journal of the American Medical Association,* 270, 2207–2212.

Miller, V. P., Ernst, C., and Collins, F. (1999). Smoking-attributable medical costs in the USA. *Social Science and Medicine,* 48, 375–391.

Morbidity and Mortality Weekly. (1998). Tobacco use among high school students — United States, 1997. *Morbidity and Mortality Weekly,* 229–233.

Peto, R., Lopez, A. D., Boreham, J., Thun, M., and Heath, C. (1994). *Mortality from smoking in developed countries, 1950–2000.* New York: Oxford University Press.

Pierce, J. P., and Gilpin, E. (1996). How long will today's new adolescent smoker be addicted to cigarettes? *American Journal of Public Health, 86,* 253–256.

Ribisl, K. M., Williams, R. S., and Kim, A. E. (2003). Internet sales of cigarettes to minors. *Journal of the American Medical Association,* 290(10), 1356–1359.

Smith, C., and Faris, R. (2002). *Religion and American adolescent delinquency, risk behaviors and constructive social activities.* Chapel Hill, NC: National Study of Youth and Religion.

Spangler, J. G., Bell, R. A., Knick, S., Michielutte, R., Dignan, M. B., and Summerson, J. H. (1998). Church-related correlates of tobacco use among Lumbee Indians in North Carolina. *Ethnicity and Disease,* 8(1), 73–80.

Spurgeon, D. (1999). Studies reveal increased smoking among students in Canada. *British Medical Journal,* 319 (7222), 1391.

Workaholism

"He often worked 70-hour weeks"

After their monthly board meeting at church, Joe Fulton lingered until everyone but Rev. Keith Samson had left. This was something different since Joe was usually the first one out the door — off to take a run, mow his lawn, or catch up on something at work. Today, however, he wanted to talk to Keith alone. "Allison has seen an attorney. She wants a divorce. I don't know what I am going to do." Keith was surprised, both by that news, and by the fact that Joe was sharing something so personal. He was usually very talkative, pleasant, and friendly, but in the past he had always kept their interactions on a rather superficial level.

Keith had known Joe for years as a member of the congregation and as a trusted elder of the church. He had worked closely with him over the years and knew him to be a hard worker, dedicated, and responsible. He often referred to him as a "go-the-extra-mile" kind of guy. Now for the first time he was seeing Joe vulnerable and at a loss as to what to do. Most strikingly different was that Joe was asking for, or at least implying that he wanted, help. Keith recognized that Joe was at a turning point in his life. **Pastoral Assessment**

Joe's father was a laborer who had eventually started his own construction company. He worked long hours and often was not home when Joe was a child. Joe's mother was a registered nurse who did shift **Relevant History** work. Joe and his brother were often left with one of many babysitters who came and went in their lives. When Joe was about eight years old, he was often left alone with his brother, who was two years younger. Joe took care of their needs as best he could by making sure they both had meals, went to bed on time, and got off to school in the mornings if no one else was around. Their parents separated twice and finally divorced when Joe was 13. He stayed with his father, and his brother went with his mother, who moved out of state to take a job and "start a new life." Joe saw her only about once a year after that. His mother had been neither abusive nor nurturing. His father, though they lived in the same house, was as emotionally distant as his mother was geographically distant. Joe's father was critical of Joe — for running track in high school instead of playing football, for getting Bs and Cs instead of being on the honor roll, for not washing the car well enough, and for generally not living up to his standards, which seemed to change and expand at a rate that eluded Joe. After Joe's mother left, his father was around even less. He never attended a track meet to watch his son. Neither parent acknowledged Joe's fourteenth birthday, and when he mentioned his birthday later to his father, he realized that his dad did not even know when it was. Throughout his childhood and adolescence, Joe attended youth activities with a neighborhood friend at the friend's church; he derived some of the nurturing and acceptance missing at home from this and continued his church involvement as an adult.

Joe went to college and worked in the local store of a national chain sporting goods company throughout the last three years. After graduation, he continued at the store, gradually working his way up the career ladder to assistant store manager, manager, and then to a regional manager. His success in business was the one thing that earned his father's praise. He married Allison when she was 33 and he was 36. They had their first child two years later, and she was now pregnant again. Joe's father died five years ago, and his mother still lived out of state and visited with them about once a year. Joe had served as an elder for several years, and with his business background and experience he quite willingly and capably took on responsibilities related to the business functioning of the church. He often worked 70-hour weeks, including late nights, weekends, and paperwork and phone calls at home. Between work, church business, and running for exercise he had little time left to spend with Allison and his son. Allison repeatedly asked him over the years to change what she called his "workaholic" behavior, but despite promises to change, Joe's behavior continued. During the past six months Allison had not once even broached the subject with him. She had, in essence, given up.

The term "workaholism" was coined in the late 1960s by Wayne Oates, a minister and professor of the psychology of religion (as cited in McMillan et al., 2004). Almost four decades later, the elements and dimensions of workaholism are still not clearly defined in a way that is universally recognized by the lay public and consistently used by researchers on the topic (see Burke, 1999, for further discussion). The concept of workaholism has been addressed in magazine articles (see Klein, 2005; Sachs, 2003; Tucker, 2004), multiple self-help books (see the Resources list at the end of the chapter), and in self-help articles in professional journals (Nowicki and Summers, 2005). Though the term and notion of workaholism are prevalent in our culture, the definitions and beliefs about its effects vary. While most of those who write on workaholism conceptualize it as having multiple negative effects, some recent data suggest that it does not *necessarily* have negative effects on intimate relationships, and that a partner might provide a stress-buffering support system for the workaholic (McMillan et al., 2004). No official diagnostic criteria exist for patterns of excessive work behavior and its related effects, but definitions of workaholism used by researchers and writers include the following concepts:

Diagnostic Criteria

- excessive focus on work and overwork behavior that is not driven by financial need (Killinger, 1991; McMillan et al., 2002);

- difficulty disengaging from thinking about or engaging in work (McMillan et al., 2004);

- addictive-like symptoms and behaviors (hence the play on the word "alcoholism") such as self-medicating emotional pain by over-working, denial of related problems, associated highs and lows of mood related to "work binges," irritability, anxiety, and depression (Robinson and Kelley, 1998; Killinger, 1991);

- obsessions and compulsions related to work behavior (Robinson, 2000);

- related relationship problems (Burke, 1999; Robinson and Kelley, 1998);

- lack of balance in one's life (Killinger, 1991);

- low levels of work enjoyment (Spence and Robbins, 1992);

- exclusion of other life activities (Robinson, 2001);

- distress or guilt when not working;

- negative psychological and/or physical health (Spence and Robbins, 1992); and

- impaired self-image, poor self-esteem, control issues, competitive-ness, and an escape from or avoidance of unpleasant life situations or one's feelings (as cited in Seybold and Salmone, 1994).

Several types of workaholic behavior patterns have been described in the literature, including compulsive-dependent, perfectionist, achievement-oriented (Scott et al., 1997), and workaholics, enthusiasts, and enthusiastic workaholics (Spence and Robbins, 1992). The type of workaholic pattern determines the effects of the related behaviors.

Scales to assess "work addiction" or workaholism have been created for research and for self-assessment purposes. The workaholism

Battery, Revised (Work BAT-R; McMillan et al., 2002) is a 14-item questionnaire that is a revised version of the workaholism Battery (Spence and Robbins, 1992). The revised battery is a research tool. In a study in New Zealand it was used to identify workaholics based on two factors — "enjoyment" (of work, so one has difficultly not working) and "drive" (feeling obligated to work). The Work Addiction Risk Test (WART) is a 25-item self-report inventory to help individuals measure their work behavior (Robinson, 1998). Workaholics Anonymous has a 20-item self-assessment tool on its website (Workaholics Anonymous, 2005). The Workaholic Quiz is a 30-item inventory (Killinger, 1991). These self-report scales assess one's work related behaviors, attitudes, feelings, and the effects on one's life.

Response to Vignette

Though the marital problems related to Joe's excessive work behavior and other commitments had been ongoing for years, it took his wife's dramatic action of seeing a divorce lawyer to enable him to really hear what she had been saying for years — that work, running, and church responsibilities were his priorities and she and their family were not. Allison had been feeling ignored and rejected as well as overburdened with carrying the parenting and family responsibilities. Words had not been sufficient to alarm him or spur him to change his behavior, but her recent action was. It jolted Joe into the realization of the severity of her dissatisfaction with their lives together. He loved her and responded to the threat and very real possibility of losing his marriage and family by talking to Keith, and then taking his advice to seek professional help.

Allison was encouraged by Joe's response and readily agreed to be involved in the counseling sessions with him. Joe initially worked separately with the therapist; then later they had a couple of joint sessions in which the therapist helped them both express, listen, clarify, problem-solve, and plan for their futures.

Treatment within the Faith Community

Joe had known Keith for years and had worked with him on many church-related projects; they had an established trusting relationship. Building relationships with members of the congregation had long been the cornerstone of Keith's approach to effective pastoral counseling. Because of personal relationships, trust, and rapport built gradually over time, church members often felt comfortable approaching Keith with their personal as well as spiritual concerns. He had the reputation of being available, compassionate, trustworthy, and nonjudgmental. So when Joe finally became aware of his marital crisis, the first person he turned to was his pastor.

Keith listened, gave Joe objective feedback, and encouraged him to explore his reasons for continually keeping himself so busy and the effects of his current lifestyle. Keith provided Joe with names of several psychologists. Now motivated by a crisis in his life, Joe scheduled an appointment with one of them. Keith also provided Joe with several related self-help books from the church library. The library continued to grow as church members passed through Keith's doors with many and varied problems. He purchased books to educate himself in order to be better equipped to help his parishioners and to have them available for lending. In addition, as Joe progressed in his therapy, Keith helped him follow his new goal of limiting his church-related commitments to a reasonable amount of time — enough involvement that Joe remained able to keep his church connections, but not enough to contribute to an unbalanced life. He also helped Joe choose church activities that included Allison and their son, in order to help foster, not detract from, his family life.

Indications for Referral

Treatment by a mental health professional is recommended if a person exhibits significant obsessive-compulsive traits, depressive or anxiety symptoms, or significant relationship problems. Referrals for counseling might also be appropriate for family members of workaholics who are significantly affected by the person's behavior. Counseling for those associated with workaholics would focus not on the workaholic's behavior, but on the thoughts, feelings, and behavior of the partner, spouse, or child of the workaholic (Seybold and Salomone, 1994).

Therapy will occur only if a workaholic recognizes the dysfunctional behaviors and wants to make personal changes, or if significant relationships are so negatively affected that the person decides to address that problem. Robinson and colleagues (2001) recommend that marriage and family therapists routinely screen for workaholism as a contributing factor to the presenting problem. Interviews as well as screening inventories can be used for this purpose.

Treatment by Mental Health Specialist

Ten warning signs garnered from case studies can be used to help therapists identify "work addiction":

1. hurrying and staying busy
2. need to control
3. perfectionism
4. difficulty with relationships
5. work binges
6. difficulty relaxing and having fun
7. not remembering conversations because of exhaustion or preoccupation with work-related thoughts; tuning out the present
8. impatience and irritability
9. feelings of self-inadequacy
10. self-neglect (Robinson and Kelley, 1998).

Once the "work addiction" behavior is identified as problematic, treatment goals are to decrease or eliminate the associated dysfunctional *thoughts* and to modify *behavior* to create a balance between meaningful work, healthy leisure activities, and personal and spiritual time (Burwell and Chen, 2002; Robinson, 2000). Specific cognitive behavior therapy techniques such as rational emotive behavior therapy

(REBT) are suggested for workaholics (Burwell and Chen, 2002). This approach entails helping the client identify his or her irrational *beliefs* and self-defeating *thoughts* (as opposed to life events) as the source of the problem, to dispute the beliefs and thoughts, and then learn to replace them with more effective, accurate, and life-enhancing ones (Albert Ellis Institute, 2005).

Since the family system can contribute to the development and maintenance of the workaholism of a family member, family involvement in the counseling process might be indicated (Seybold and Salomone, 1994). The behavior does not exist in a vacuum, and so addressing other family members' (especially the spouse's) roles in a dysfunctional family system might be important. The workaholism should not automatically be assumed to be the cause of problems, but might instead be a response to (i.e., an escape from) other problems in one's life. However, based on their research, McMillan and colleagues (2004) caution against assuming that workaholism always negatively affects a relationship. They recommend assessing the level of matching between the partners, and suggest that if both are workaholics, the negative impact of the workaholism is less.

Joe's therapist first helped him clarify, articulate, and prioritize his values. As a result of that process he came to realize that although work is important to him, it is not the most important thing in his life. Allison and his marriage, their son, and their expected baby were in fact more important. He also realized that leisure time, fun, reading, family vacations, church, and socializing with friends were all very important to him — although he had not been taking the time to actually enjoy these. The main area of focus for Joe in therapy was the verbal abuse and lack of emotional support and nurturing in his childhood, and the resultant ways of thinking and interpreting his world. He processed everything through a set of beliefs that others were unaware of because his behaviors signaled the opposite. In fact, until therapy he was not totally aware of the prevalence of his dysfunctional thinking and self-talk. Experiences from his childhood that were not intended by his parents to be harmful were understandably perceived by him in ways that were psychologically injurious and were translated by him into dysfunctional ways of thinking — "I'm not important," "I'm not good enough," "I should be better," "I'm not really loveable," "Don't get too close to people you love," and "Money equals success." The patterns that emerged for Joe were avoidance of intimacy and relationships (in an attempt to spare himself emotional pain from being left, rejected, or ignored as he was in his childhood); competitiveness (with others at work, where he continually tried to do well in order to be recognized by his bosses, with himself in always trying to increase the distance he ran each week); giving (of material things to his family and through his hours spent on church business), and workaholism. He was in effect trying to prove that he was good enough — seeking the approval of his wife, bosses, neighbors, congregation, and, as he came to realize, his father (even though he had been dead for years). So everything was an effort — and judged by himself to be not enough or not good enough. This perpetuated a pattern of trying harder, which led to more avoidance, competition, buying, providing, volunteering, and ultimately to Allison's filing for divorce.

Once he recognized his inaccurate and ineffective thoughts, he began challenging them. He realized that he had been behaving as if these things were true even though, as he discovered when therapy shined a light on them, they were not. He learned to "think about his thinking," and when he caught himself responding to the well-ingrained, but inaccurate thoughts, he consciously examined them and modified them to more accurate and functional ways of thinking about himself and his life (such as "Allison loves me," "being happy equals success," "I am happy doing many things in addition to work," "I don't have to prove myself to anyone"). This led to more self-acceptance, less need to "prove" himself, and therefore a decreased need to be busy. The therapist also helped Joe develop a specific plan to change his behaviors and thereby test, validate, and strengthen his new rational cognitions. His plan set a limit on work hours, included a once-a-month "date" with his wife, built in family recreation time, set limits on volunteer church work, and set times for exercising that included his running but also included walks and going swimming with the family or playing ball with his son. With a conscious effort on his part and help from Allison and Keith to make changes and stay on track, Joe was able to make life-changing adjustments to his thinking and behavior. Once established, these changes were easy for him to maintain, because the rewards of a happier, more balanced life reinforced him for doing so.

Cross-Cultural Issues   Work is highly valued in many if not all cultures. But few if any studies of workaholism have been conducted to explore racial, cultural, or geographic differences in workaholic type behaviors (Robinson, 2000a). Most of the information that is available is related to workaholism in males. The Chartered Institute of Personnel and Development in Great Britain surveyed nearly 300 people who worked more than 48 hours per week; 82 percent of these longer-hour workers were male (Higginbottom, 2002).

Several Japanese studies (as cited in Robinson, 2000b) have suggested that chronic and excessive work and related stress can lead to psychological, physical, and interpersonal problems. The Japanese language has a word, *karoshi,* for the not uncommon occurrence of death (generally from stroke or heart attack) that is related to overwork by Japanese men (Robinson, 2000b).

Resources   Workaholics Anonymous, World Service Organization (WA); P.O. Box 289, Menlo Park, CA 94026-0289; (510) 273-9253; *www.workaholics-anonymous.org*; started in 1983 to help others who are affected by their own or others' excessive work behavior. The website provides a questionnaire ("How Do I Know If I'm a Workaholic?"), the 12 steps of Workaholics Anonymous, "Tools of Recovery" (a list of self-help strategies), and a national list of meetings.

Workaholic International Network; 2609 Surfwood Drive, Las Vegas, NV 89128; (702) 838-6056; *www.workaholic.org*; a light-hearted, humorous website that offers on-line newsletters and articles and links to related websites.

Calling It a Day: Daily Meditation for Workaholics (Robert Larranaga, San Francisco: Harper and Row, 1990).

Chained to the Desk: A Guidebook for Workaholics, Their Partners and Children, and the Clinicians Who Treat Them (Bryan E. Robinson, New York: New York University Press, 1998).

The Man Who Mistook His Job for a Life: A Chronic Overachiever Finds the Way Home (Jonathon Lazear, New York: Crown Publishers, 2001).

Time Out: Daily Devotions for Workaholics (Gary E. Hurst, Mike Kachura, and Larry D. Sides, Nashville: Thomas Nelson Publishers, 1991).

Who's Driving Your Bus? Codependent Business Behaviors of Workaholics, Perfectionists, Martyrs, Tap Dancers, Caretakers, and People-Pleasers (Earnie Larsen and Jeanette Goodstein, San Diego: Pfeiffer and Company, 1993).

Work to Live (Joe Robinson, New York: Perigee Books, 2003).

Workaholics: The Respectable Addicts (Barbara Killinger, Buffalo: Firefly Books, 1991).

Helpful Books

Albert Ellis Institute (AEI) website. (2005). Retrieved August 20, 2005, from *www.rebt.org*.

Burke, R. J. (1999). Workaholism and extra-work satisfactions. *International Journal of Organizational Analysis, 7,* 352–364.

Burwell, R., and Chen, C. P. (2002). Applying REBT to workaholic clients. *Counseling Psychology Quarterly, 15,* 219–228.

Higginbottom, K. (2002). Workers shun holidays. *People Management, 8,* 13.

References

Killinger, B. (1991). *Workaholics: The respectable addicts*. Buffalo, NY: Firefly.

Klein, J. M. (2005, March/April). Busy at work, ducking the kids? *Psychology Today, 38,* 30.

McMillan, L. H. W., Brady, E. C., O'Driscoll, M. P., and Marsh, N. V. (2002). A multifaceted validation study of Spence and Robbins's (1992) workaholism battery. *Journal of Occupational and Organizational Psychology, 75,* 357–368.

McMillan, L. H. W., O'Driscoll, M. P., and Brady, E. C. (2004). The impact of workaholism on personal relationships. *British Journal of Guidance and Counselling, 32,* 171–186.

Nowicki, M., and Summers, J. (2005). Managing the workaholic (in you!). *Healthcare Financial Management, 59,* 98–102.

Oates, W. E. (1968). On being a 'workaholic' (a serious jest). *Pastoral Psychology, 19,* 16–20.

Robinson, B. E. (1998). *Chained to the desk*. New York: New York University Press.

Robinson, B. E. (2000a). A typology of workaholics with implications for counselors. *Journal of Addictions and Offender Counseling, 21,* 34–48.

Robinson, B. E. (2000b). Workaholism: Bridging the gap between workplace, sociocultural, and family research. *Journal of Employment Counseling, 37,* 31–47.

Robinson, B. E. (2001). Workaholism and family functioning: A profile of familial relationships, psychological outcomes, and research considerations. *Contemporary Family Therapy: An International Journal, 23,* 123–135.

Robinson, B. E., Carroll, J. J., and Flowers, C. (2001). Marital estrangement, positive affect, and locus of control among spouses of workaholics and spouses of nonworkaholics: A national study. *American Journal of Family Therapy, 29,* 397–410.

Robinson, B. E., and Kelley, L. (1998). Adult children of workaholics: Self-concept, anxiety, depression, and locus of control. *American Journal of Family Therapy,* 26, 223–238.

Sachs, A. (2003, April 7). Workaholics, reform! *Time,* 161 (14), 87.

Scott, K. S., Moore, K. S., and Miceli, M. P. (1997). An exploration of the meaning and consequences of workaholism. *Human Relations,* 50, 287–314.

Seybold, K. C., and Salomone, P. R. (1994). Understanding workaholism: A review of causes and counseling approaches. *Journal of Counseling and Development,* 73, 4–9.

Spence, J. T., and Robbins, A. S. (1992). Workaholism: Definition, measurement, and preliminary results. *Journal of Personality Assessment,* 58, 160–178.

Tucker, R. (2004, October 4). These ads are all work and no play. *Fortune,* 150 (7), 52.

Workaholics Anonymous. How do I know if I'm a workaholic? Retrieved July 29, 2005, from *www.workaholics-anonymous.org.*

Summary
and Conclusions

Religion plays an essential role in the lives of individuals and their families, especially when facing difficult matters. Given that clergy are often the first professionals sought for help with personal problems, including addictions and compulsions, those in ministry need to understand the key concerns to be addressed. Information is needed about how to diagnose and assess problems, types of treatment that can be initiated in the faith community, when referral is required, and to whom to refer. This volume identifies 17 addictions and compulsions, provides illustrative cases, lists resources available, and suggests when and from whom to seek additional professional assistance. There is an emphasis on self-help resources available on the Internet.

Because of the valued role that religion plays in the lives of many, it is essential that pastors, chaplains, parish nurses, and others in ministry be knowledgeable about the addictions that affect individuals and the families they serve. Religious faith is a primary, positive coping strategy for many persons who face these issues. Faith communities can have a positive role by providing accurate information for individuals regarding addictions. Congregations often have long-established communication networks that allow them to stay in touch with members in need of education and support on this subject and other health concerns. Accurate information about addictions and compulsions can be disseminated through these networks.

Pastoral care is a responsibility of the whole religious community. Clergy can offer guidance and direction, but the task of caring for those suffering from addictions requires a larger group of helpers. Much emphasis is given to prevention through education within the community of faith. The book offers concrete suggestions about how the issues addressed can be understood as forms of ministry for the entire congregation.

Glossary

Abstinence: To refrain from the usage of substances to which a person has become addicted.

Abuse: The harmful use of a substance.

Addiction: A state of dependence based on tolerance (a need for increased amounts of the substance for intoxication to occur or lessened effect with the same amount of substance), withdrawal symptoms or using to avoid withdrawal symptoms, an inability to control the use, and/or the substance use is having a negative effect on one's social, occupational, or recreational life or on one's physical or psychological health.

Al-Anon: An association dedicated to helping the families of alcoholics through a support group and 12-step program.

Alcoholics Anonymous: The group that developed the 12-step approach to recovery from alcohol addiction (alcoholism). Many other groups have adapted this method to help people recover from other addictions, for example, Narcotics Anonymous and Cocaine Anonymous.

Amphetamines: A group of synthetic substances that have a powerful stimulant effect on the central nervous system. On the street, amphetamines are often referred to as "speed."

Anxiety: The state of feeling apprehension, agitation, uncertainty, and fear at the thought of some future or uncertain event or situation.

Barbiturates: A class of drugs used medically to promote sleep or sedation. They act as central nervous system depressants and are subject to abuse.

Benzodiazepines: The so-called "minor" tranquilizers, central nervous system depressants prescribed to relieve anxiety and produce sleep. Benzodiazepines include tranquilizers such as diazepam (Valium) and alprazolam (Xanax), as well as sleeping pills such as flurazepam (Dalmane) and triazolam (Halcion).

Binge: Uninterrupted consumption of a drug for several hours or days.

Blackout: A period of memory loss for which there is no recall of activities as a result of alcohol or other drug abuse.

Buprenorphine: A new medication awaiting FDA approval for treatment of opioid addiction. It blocks the effects of opioids on the brain.

Cannabis: The botanical name for the plant from which marijuana comes.

Central Nervous System: The brain and spinal cord.

Chemical Dependency: Physical or psychological reliance on drugs.

Coca: The plant from which cocaine is derived.

Cocaine: A highly addictive stimulant drug derived from the coca plant, which produces profound feelings of pleasure.

Codeine: A natural opioid compound that is a relatively weak, but effective.

Cognitive: Having to do with the ability to think or reason; sometimes used to describe memory process; the operation of the mind as distinct from emotions.

Cognitive behavior therapy: A form of psychological therapy that focuses on directly modifying both thought process and behavior.

Compulsion: An intrusive, repetitive, and unwanted urge to perform an act that is counter to a person's usual conduct. Compulsion contrasts with obsession, which is an involuntary repetition of a purely mental process such as a thought, daydream, image, or emotion.

Consciousness: Our own awareness of ourselves and the world; the mental processes that we can perceive; our thoughts and feelings.

Controlled substances: Psychoactive substances whose distribution is forbidden by law or limited to scientific, medical, or pharmaceutical channels.

Coping skills: Refers to an individual's abilities to deal with stress and difficulties. An individual with well-developed coping skills will have increased resilience to deal with stressful situations.

Crack: Slang term for a smokable form of cocaine.

Craving: A powerful, often uncontrollable desire.

Delusions: Fixed, false beliefs from which an individual cannot be dissuaded.

Denial: Refusing to admit that someone is addicted or accepting the degree of harm caused by an addiction.

Depressants: Drugs that relieve anxiety and produce sleep. Depressants include barbiturates, benzodiazepines, and alcohol.

Detoxification: A process of withdrawing a person from a psychoactive substance in a safe manner.

***Diagnostic and Statistical Manual of Mental Disorders,* 4th ed., text revision (DSM-IV-TR):** The official manual of mental health problems developed by the American Psychiatric Association. This reference book is used by mental health professionals to understand and diagnose psychological problems.

Dissociation: The process whereby thoughts and ideas can be split off from consciousness and may function independently.

Dopamine: A neurotransmitter present in regions of the brain that regulate movement, emotion, motivation, and the feeling of pleasure.

Downers: Slang name for barbiturates, minor tranquilizers, and related depressants.

Ecstasy (MDMA): A chemically modified amphetamine that has hallucinogenic, as well as stimulant, properties.

Enabling: Any action by another person that intentionally or unintentionally has the effect of facilitating the continuation of an individual's addictive process.

Flashback: A recurrence of certain aspects of a person's drug experience without the user having taken the drug for weeks, months, or even years afterward.

Hallucinations: Abnormal perceptions which occur as symptoms of schizophrenia or other severe forms of mental illness; mostly in the form of hearing voices or seeing objects.

Hashish: The concentrated resin of the cannabis plant.

Heroin: A potent, widely abused opiate that produces a profound addiction. It consists of two morphine molecules linked together chemically.

Hormone: A chemical substance formed in glands in the body and carried in the blood to organs and tissues, where it influences function, structure, and behavior.

Impairment: A dysfunctional state resulting from the use of psychoactive substances.

Inhalant: Any drug administered by breathing in its vapors. Most abused inhalants are organic solvents such as glue and paint thinner, or anesthetic gases such as ether and nitrous oxide.

Mescaline: A naturally occurring hallucinogenic drug that acts on the serotonin receptor in the brain.

Methadone: A long-lasting synthetic opiate used to treat heroin addiction.

Methamphetamine: A commonly abused potent stimulant drug that is part of a larger family of amphetamines.

Morphine: The most potent natural opiate compound produced by the opium poppy.

Neuron: A nerve cell in the brain.

Neurotransmitter: Chemicals produced by neurons to carry their messages to other neurons.

Nicotine: The drug in tobacco that is addictive.

Obsession: Having recurrent thoughts about something or someone that are difficult to stop or control.

Organic solvents: A class of inhalants that includes substances such as gasoline, paint thinner, and glue.

Outpatient treatment: Nonresidential medical care where patients live at home, often work, and come to a clinic for treatment.

Overdose: The condition that results when too much of a drug is taken, making a person sick or unconscious and sometimes resulting in a serious toxic reaction and death.

Paranoid thinking: Exaggerated belief or suspicion that one is being persecuted, harassed, or unfairly treated.

Physical dependence: This term is often used to mean the same thing as addiction. It can be thought of in two ways: (1) psychological feelings of discomfort when the drug is not available (psychological dependence), or (2) a state where the body requires the regular use of alcohol or other drugs in order to continue to function (physical dependence). If a person develops physical dependence and then stops taking the drug, he or she is likely to experience withdrawal symptoms.

Polydrug user: An individual who uses more than one drug.

Prescription drug abuse: The intentional misuse of a medication outside of the normally accepted standards of its use.

Prevention: Measures aimed at stopping drug abuse before it starts.

Psilocybin: A natural hallucinogenic drug derived from a mushroom.

Psychedelic drug: A drug that distorts perception, thought, and feeling. This term is typically used to refer to drugs with actions like those of LSD.

Psychiatrist: A physician who has special training (medical residency in psychiatry) to handle psychological problems. A psychiatrist can hospitalize patients and may treat with medications, psychotherapy, or both.

Psychoactive drug: A drug that affects the brain in such a way as to alter consciousness.

Psychological dependence: Mental or emotional feelings of discomfort when a drug of choice is not available.

Psychologist: A doctor with an advanced degree (Ph.D. or Psy.D.) who is trained to use a variety of treatment modalities including individual and group psychotherapy, cognitive therapy, behavior modification, psychodynamic psychotherapy, and family systems. She or he also does psychological testing.

Psychopharmacology: The management of mental illness using medication.

Psychosis: A severe mental illness characterized by loss of contact with reality.

Psychotherapy: A process in which an individual seeks to resolve problems or achieve psychological growth through oral communication with a mental health professional.

Relapse: The return to drinking or other psychoactive substance use after a period of abstinence or moderate use.

Rock: Slang name for a small amount of crack cocaine in a solid form.

Run: A binge of uninterrupted consumption of a drug for several hours or days.

Rush: Intense feelings of pleasure that rapidly follow the taking of some drugs.

Sobriety: Total abstinence from substance use by an addicted individual.

Social worker (M.S.W.): A mental health professional who is trained to understand and emphasize the effect of environmental factors on mental problems. They often assist individuals and their families in locating and accessing available community services.

Stimulants: A class of drugs that elevates mood, increases feelings of well-being, and increases energy and alertness. Stimulants include cocaine, methamphetamine, and methylphenidate (Ritalin).

Stress: Tension resulting from a person's response to his or her environment.

Substance abuse: Excess, abnormal, or illegal use of drugs or alcohol.

Tolerance: A condition in which higher doses of a drug are required to produce the same effect as during initial use.

Tranquilizers: Depressant prescription drugs that relieve anxiety.

Uppers: Slang name for stimulants.

Withdrawal: Symptoms that occur after chronic use of a drug is reduced or stopped.

Index

(Terms in **bold face** can be found in the resource, bibliography, or glossary sections.)